GREAT SPORTS TEAMS

THE DALLAS COWBOYS

JOHN F. GRABOWSKI

Lucent Books, San Diego, CA

796.332
GRA

On cover: Emmitt Smith

ᴊᴍ TH
Library of Congress Cataloging-in-Publication Data

Grabowski, John F.
 The Dallas Cowboys / by John F. Grabowski.
  p. cm. — (Great sports teams in history)
 Includes bibliographical references and index.
 Summary: Discusses the history of the Cowboys
football team and the lives and careers of Coach Tom
Landry and players Bob Lilly, Bob Hayes, Roger
Staubach, Tony Dorsett, Troy Aikman, and Emmitt Smith.
 ISBN 1-56006-939-2 (hardback : alk. paper)
 1. Dallas Cowboys (Football team)—History—Juvenile
literature. 2. Football players—United States—Biography—
Juvenile literature. [1. Dallas Cowboys (Football team)—
History. 2. Football—History. 3. Football players.] I. Title.
II. Series.
 GV956.D3 G73 2002
 796.332'64'097642812—dc21

2001002789

Copyright © 2002 by Lucent Books, Inc.
10911 Technology Place, San Diego, CA 92127
Printed in the U.S.A.

Contents

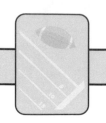

FOREWORD

Former Supreme Court Chief Justice Warren Burger once said he always read the sports section of the newspaper first because it was about humanity's successes, while the front page listed only humanity's failures. Millions of people across the country today would probably agree with Burger's preference for tales of human endurance, record-breaking performances, and feats of athletic prowess. Although these accomplishments are far beyond what most Americans can ever hope to achieve, average people, the fans, do want to affect what happens on the field of play. Thus, their role becomes one of encouragement. They cheer for their favorite players and team and boo the opposition.

ABC Sports president Roone Arledge once attempted to explain the relationship between fan and team. Sport, said Arledge, is "a set of created circumstances—artificial circumstances—set up to frustrate a man in pursuit of a goal. He has to have certain skills to overcome those obstacles—or even to challenge them. And people who don't have those skills cheer him and admire him." Over a period of time, the admirers may develop a rabid—even irrational—allegiance to a particular team. Indeed, the word "fan" itself is derived from the word "fanatic," someone possessed by an excessive and irrational zeal. Sometimes this devotion to a team is because of a favorite player; often it's because of where a person lives, and, occasionally, it's because of a family allegiance to a particular club.

Whatever the reason, the bond formed between team and fan often defies reason. It may be easy to understand the appeal of the New York Yankees, a team that has gone to the World Series an incredible thirty seven times and won twenty six championships, nearly three times as many as any other major league baseball team. It is more difficult, though, to comprehend the fanaticism of Chicago Cubs fans, who faithfully follow the progress of a team that hasn't won a World Series since 1908. Regardless, the Cubs have surpassed the 2 million mark in home attendance in 14 of the last 17 years. In fact, their two highest totals were posted in 1999 and 2000, when the team finished in last place.

Each volume in Lucent's *Great Sports Teams in History* series examines a team that has left its mark on the American sports consciousness. Each book looks at the history and tradition of the club in an attempt to understand its appeal and the loyalty—even passion—of its fans. Each volume also examines the lives and careers of people who played significant roles in the team's history. Players, managers, coaches, and front office executives are represented.

Footnoted quotations help bring the text in each book to life. In addition, all books include an annotated bibliography and a For Further Reading list to supply students with sources for conducting additional individual research.

No one volume can hope to explain fully the mystique of the New York Yankees, Boston Celtics, Dallas Cowboys, or Montreal Canadiens. The Lucent *Great Sports Teams in History* series, however, gives interested readers a solid start on the road to understanding the mysterious bond that exists between modern professional sports teams and their devoted followers.

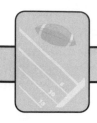

INTRODUCTION

A Larger-than-Life Mystique

Some say everything is bigger in Texas. That may or may not be true, but it certainly is so in the natives' love of football. Texans take their football seriously. The sport has a lengthy, storied history, with the area around Dallas and Fort Worth long being one of the hotbeds of college football in the nation. Programs such as those at the University of Texas, Southern Methodist University, Texas Christian University, Texas A&M, Baylor, and Rice arouse the passions of fans who come out week after week to watch their teams perform. Players such as Sammy Baugh, Doak Walker, Kyle Rote, and Bobby Layne attended these schools and became local and national college football heroes.

When it came time for them to enter the pro ranks, however, they were forced to go outside Texas. For many years the nearest National Football League (NFL) franchise was in Washington, D.C. The old New York Yankees football franchise was transplanted to Texas to become the Dallas Texans in 1952, but the team had no local heroes to attract fans. In addition, it was the worst team in the league. The combination proved fatal. After just seven games, owner Ted Collins was forced to return the financially impoverished franchise to the league. It finished out its lone season as a road team out of Hershey, Pennsylvania, compiling a record of 1-11.

Despite the team's poor attendance figures in Dallas, Texas oilman Clint Murchison Jr. thought he could make the team a success there. He asked the NFL if he could buy the club and return it to his home state. NFL commissioner Bert Bell, however, sold the team instead to his old friend Carroll Rosenbloom. The next year the club was reborn as the Baltimore Colts.

Sammy Baugh became a local and national college football hero for his performance in Texas athletics.

NFL commissioner Bert Bell, right, refused to sell the Dallas Texans to Texas oilman Clint Murchison Jr.

Murchison never gave up the idea of bringing a professional team back to Texas, however. He finally succeeded when the Dallas Cowboys came to life in 1960. The rest, as they say, is history.

From their expansionist beginnings, the Cowboys have grown into one of the most profitable franchises on the professional sports scene. Their success has been due to a combination of things, including great players, great coaching, and great promotion.

College football is still wildly popular in Texas, as is the high school game. But professional football now stands tall alongside them. Native Texans like Bob Lilly and Tom Landry—together with "imports" like Bob Hayes, Roger Staubach, and Emmitt Smith—have helped build a tradition that has made the Dallas Cowboys one of the most successful franchises in all of sports. Their wide-open style of play, with marquee players at key positions, has helped endear them to a nation desperate for fast-moving action from its larger-than-life heroes.

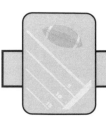

CHAPTER 1

America's Team

In little more than a decade the Dallas Cowboys were transformed from a newly formed expansion team into champions of the National Football League. They became a league powerhouse, fueled by explosive players who captured the public's imagination with their exploits on the field and led by an unflappable coach who paced the sidelines with no outward show of emotion. Gradually their appeal spread from the Dallas area across the entire nation. Fans everywhere began rooting for the former underdogs who showed what could be achieved through hard work and determination. They evolved from being Dallas's team to America's Team. That this transformation took place in such a relatively short time makes it all the more amazing, particularly when the team's rocky beginning is taken into account.

The Beginning

In 1958 the Baltimore Colts defeated the New York Giants in overtime 23-17 to win the National Football League championship. What is usually referred to as "The Greatest Game Ever Played," because of its drama and the fact that it was played before a national television audience, helped change the face of professional football. As the pro game reached new heights of popularity, rumors of NFL expansion first began to be heard. Chicago Bears owner George Halas headed a committee formed by the league to examine expansion possibilities. The committee proposed that two new teams be added to the league, to begin play with the 1961 season. One of these franchises would be located in Dallas, the other in either Houston or Minneapolis.

These plans were changed, however, when Texas millionaire Lamar Hunt announced that the newly formed American Football League would begin play in 1960. The league was to consist of eight teams, with clubs in both Dallas and Houston.

Upon hearing this news, Halas began to push for the NFL's immediate expansion in hopes of beating the new league to the untouched Texas market. He was able to find a group of men willing

Tex Schramm, left, Pete Roselle, middle, and Lamar Hunt, right, participate in a committee to decide the future of professional football.

to back a team in Dallas. The group was headed by Clint Murchison Jr., heir to one of Texas's largest oil fortunes, and included his brother John Murchison, Bedford Wynne, Toddie Lee Wynne, and Fritz Hawn. Knowing he needed an experienced football man to run the team, Murchison contacted Texas E. "Tex" Schramm. Tex Schramm had been general manager of the Los Angeles Rams until 1957, when he resigned to take a job with CBS Sports. He signed on as the new team's general manager and began his search for a head coach.

Growing Pains

Schramm contacted New York Giants owner Wellington Mara and received permission to speak with New York's assistant defensive coach, Tom Landry, about the coaching position. The job appealed to Landry, who liked the idea of moving back to his home state and having complete authority over the on-field operation of the team. It was a challenge he could not pass up. Landry signed a five-year contract.

On December 28, 1959, Landry was introduced to the press as the new head coach of the Dallas Rangers. (The team nickname would not be changed to the Cowboys until several weeks later.) Technically, he was now the coach of a club that had not yet been awarded a franchise, since official approval still had to be voted on by the NFL team owners at their meeting in January.

At that January meeting several NFL owners, including George Preston Marshall of the Washington Redskins, were not yet completely convinced that the league should add any new teams. Marshall did not want any team taking away part of his potential fan base in the South. It eventually took a song to make him change his tune.

Marshall had recently fired the team's band director, who had composed "Hail to the Redskins," the team's official fight song and a favorite of Marshall's. To get back at the owner, the director sold the rights to the song to a lawyer who had battled Marshall in the past. This attorney was one of Clint Murchison's lawyers. Murchison told Marshall the rights to the song would be returned to him if he approved the Dallas franchise. An agreement to that effect was reached, and on January 28, 1960, Dallas became the National Football League's first new member since its merger with the All-America Football Conference in 1950.

Don Meredith signed with the Dallas Cowboys, boosting attendance for the upstart team.

The First Season

The first order of business for the new team was obtaining players. The league's annual college draft had been held the previous November in order to give the NFL an edge over the upstart American Football League. Since the Cowboys weren't yet in existence, they could not participate. George Halas, however, had anticipated this. Before the draft, he gave Murchison permission to sign two local college stars—quarterback Don Meredith of Southern Methodist University and running back Don Perkins of the University of New Mexico—to contracts. The other owners were informed of this and did not draft the two players. In this way Dallas was assured of having a pair of local attractions to help attendance. Following the draft, Gil Brandt, the team's newly hired player/personnel director, traveled around the country signing promising college seniors who had gone undrafted.

In order to help stock the team with more experienced players, the league held another draft. Each of the established teams was allowed to protect twenty-five of the thirty-four players on its roster. The Cowboys were allowed to select three of the remaining men from each club, for a total of thirty-six players. Among the better-known names selected by Dallas were Cleveland Browns receiver Frank Clarke, New York Giants quarterback Don Heinrich, and San Francisco 49ers linebacker Jerry Tubbs. Another familiar name was added to the roster when former Washington quarterback Eddie LeBaron was obtained from the Redskins in exchange for a future draft pick.

The outlook was not especially bright for the new club (more so than nowadays, when teams can also go after well-known free agents). When all was said and done, 193 players showed up for the Cowboys' first training camp in July, at Pacific University in Forest Grove, Oregon, with hopes of winning jobs. Most were either "has-beens" or "never-weres." When the team lost its very first preseason game to the 49ers, 16-10, on August 6, it was a harbinger of things to come.

The regular season began with Dallas meeting the Pittsburgh Steelers at the Cotton Bowl in Dallas on the night of September 24. The Cowboys managed to post twenty-eight points, but the Steelers led by quarterback Bobby Layne rallied to take a 35-28 decision. Dallas's shortage of good players quickly became obvious as one loss followed another until the first week of December. After losing their first ten games the Cowboys managed to salvage a 31-31 tie with the Giants in New York's Yankee Stadium, the high point of the year for the club. However, the Cowboys finished the regular season with a record of 0-11-1, the worst record posted in league play in eighteen years. Things could only get better.

The Road to the Top

Landry added several good players to the defense for 1961, including future Hall of Fame defensive end Bob Lilly. The team also improved its talent on offense, knowing it would have to generate more excitement in order to compete with the Dallas Texans of the AFL for the fans' dollar. The changes produced immediate results. The winless club of 1960 posted victories in its first two games the next season, defeating the Steelers and the expansion Minnesota Vikings (added to the league in 1961).

As the younger players gained experience, the Cowboys began to accumulate wins. Under Landry's calm, stern guidance the Cowboys won two more games that season, then followed up with five wins in 1962. They finally reached the .500 mark in 1965 with seven wins and seven losses. "We were starting from real scratch," remembered Schramm, "and it was considered quite an accomplishment to do what we did in the first five years."[1] By that time Landry had been given an unprecedented ten-year extension on his original contract. With Murchison's solid show of support, it was now up to Landry to take the team to the next level.

Dallas's first winning season came in 1966. The Cowboys won ten games to take their first Eastern Conference title. They advanced to the NFL championship game, where they lost to the powerful Green Bay Packers. They repeated their success the following year, again losing to the Packers, this time in the memorable "Ice Bowl" game played in subzero temperatures in Green Bay, Wisconsin. In that contest the Cowboys led 17-14 with less than five minutes left in the game. Green Bay quarterback Bart Starr engineered a seventy-eight-yard drive for the winning touchdown, going over, himself, on a quarterback sneak from the 1-yard line for the final score with just sixteen seconds remaining.

By advancing further in postseason play the Cowboys were establishing themselves as one of the National Football League's best teams. However, they were also gaining a reputation as a team that could not win the "big" game. They won their division in each of the next two years but twice lost in the Eastern Conference title game. Now they were having difficulty taking that last step to winning a championship. "We lost," said general manager Schramm, "but we'd almost beaten Green Bay, with all the legends of the game. It attracted people's attention."[2]

However, with players such as Don Meredith, Bob Lilly, Don Perkins, Lee Roy Jordan, and Bob Hayes, the Cowboys were an exciting club to watch. Starting out as an expansion team, they had been underdogs for most of their existence. These factors

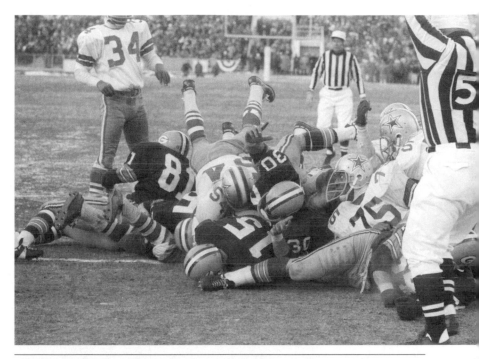

Green Bay Packers quarterback Bart Starr lunges across the goal line, stealing the "Ice Bowl" victory from Dallas.

helped Dallas win fans all across the nation. For the first time people began referring to them as America's Team. (The club's official acknowledgment of the name would not come until later, when it was used as the title of their highlight film for the 1978 season.) As Tex Schramm recalled, "We captured people's imagination because we had good-looking uniforms with that star on the helmet. We had a modest head coach that people respected. We had a snappy quarterback. We had track men playing defensive back. We were the underdog that people would be attracted to."[3]

Super Bowl Champs and More

The 1970s saw the Cowboys shed their label as losers. Their success after a decade of battling their way up from the bottom was inspirational and their appeal increased among football fans everywhere. The decade began with the team's first appearance in the Super Bowl, following the 1970 season. There, they were edged out by the Baltimore Colts, 16-13. The next year, however, they finally attained their ultimate goal.

The Cowboys began the 1971 season in a sparkling new home. Texas Stadium was christened with a 44-21 win over the New England Patriots in front of 65,708 fans on October 24. Dallas won its final seven games of the regular season on the way to compiling an 11-3 mark. The Cowboys continued on to Super Bowl VI, where they met Don Shula's Miami Dolphins. Led by quarterback Roger Staubach, they ran over the strong Miami club, emerging with a 24-3 victory and their first championship. It would not be their last.

The decade of the seventies saw the emergence of Landry's multiple-formation offense, where three, four, and sometimes five receivers might run patterns in order to confuse opponents. Staubach, runners Duane Thomas and Calvin Hill, and receivers Drew Pearson and Tony Hill led the league's most entertaining attack, an offense that would be led by stars such as Tony Dorsett, Emmitt Smith, Michael Irvin, and Troy Aikman in later years. The Doomsday Defense—the defensive unit that would be the foundation of the great Cowboys teams of the seventies—began to take shape, with Bob Lilly, Lee Roy Jordan, Chuck Howley, Mel Renfro, and Cornell Green among the stars on the other side of the ball.

The Cowboys made the playoffs for eight consecutive years before missing them in 1974. The next year the club again went to the Super Bowl, where it was beaten by the Pittsburgh Steelers, 21-17. The Cowboys won their second championship in Super Bowl XII, where they defeated the Denver Broncos, 27-10, following the 1977 season. They returned to the big game the next year in the first rematch in Super Bowl history. Playing the Pittsburgh Steelers, they duplicated their four-point loss of three years before, this time coming out on the short end of a 35-31 score in Super Bowl XIII.

Their penchant for winning brought the Cowboys more and more admirers. One did not have to live in the Dallas area to be attracted to the wide-open attack, the big-name stars, and the beautiful Dallas Cowboys cheerleaders. The club quickly cemented its reputation as one of the top teams of the era. Incredibly, from 1966 through 1985 they compiled twenty consecutive winning seasons under Landry. In his twenty-nine years as coach, they won 270 games, thirteen division titles, and made five trips to the Super Bowl.

A Change of Ownership

In 1984, as the Cowboys celebrated their twenty-fifth anniversary, the Murchison family announced the sale of the team. The original $550,000 investment was sold to an eleven-member limited partnership headed by Dallas businessman H. R. "Bum" Bright for $63 million, with the stadium adding another $20 million. The Murchison-Landry association that had brought the team to the heights of the football world had come to an end. Landry remained as head coach, but the team's remarkable run of winning seasons was coming to a close.

In 1986, the Cowboys had their first losing season since 1964, falling to 7-9 and a third-place finish in the National Football Conference's (NFC) Eastern Division. Two years later Dallas won just three games, the fewest since its winless first year of 1960. With the team's record in a downward curve, the Bright partnership sold the team to Arkansas oilman Jerry Jones for $147 million in February 1989. From the time he had bought the team five years earlier, Bright had never denied that it was solely an investment for him. "From day one," he said after the sale to Jones, "I made it clear that the Dallas Cowboys were more of a business deal for me. I do regret that we were not more successful, but it was simply time for us to sell."[4] The sale to an owner who was passionately interested in the game itself, and who was willing to spend whatever it would take to improve that team, could only have a positive effect.

Jones announced that University of Miami coach Jimmy Johnson would replace Landry as the team's head coach. At the same time, Tex Schramm announced his resignation as president and general manager of the team to become president of the new World League of American Football. The end of an era had come to Dallas Cowboys football. The team would have to rebuild in order to keep all the fans they had attracted over the years.

A Return to the Top

Jimmy Johnson had a definite plan in mind to improve the Cowboys and raise them once again to their position of prominence on the national scene. In one effort to obtain players who would bring glory back to the Dallas uniform, he began stockpiling draft picks through trades with other clubs. He made the biggest headlines by

sending star running back Herschel Walker to the Minnesota
Vikings, together with four draft picks. In exchange the Cowboys
received five players and eight draft picks. "I really didn't think it
was that much of a gamble," Johnson said. "We knew we weren't
going to be very good in 1989, and we needed a lot of help. It made
sense to take our best player and try to get as much in turn for him
as we could. We just wanted to build up draft choices and depth
and try to get better."[5] Two of the draft picks taken by the Cowboys
turned out to be running back Emmitt Smith and defensive back
Darren Woodson. With eighteen players involved, it was the largest
deal in league history. The foundation for a future contender had
been laid.

The Cowboys also became major players in the free agent market (whereby a team could go after players who were free to sign
with any team that expressed interest in them), and Jones established himself as an owner who was willing to spend big money in
order to field a winning team. He took a hands-on approach to

Owner Jerry Jones, right, and coach Jimmy Johnson, left, raised the Cowboys
back to national dominance.

running the club, saying, "This is what I do. This is not a hobby. This is my vocation and my life."[6] Such an approach had been lacking during Bright's ownership.

Although the Cowboys won just one game in 1989, the pair's first season in charge, Jones and Johnson proved to be a formidable duo. The team soon turned things around. Dallas finished 7-9 the next year and Johnson was named NFL Coach of the Year by the Associated Press. With the owner's willingness to spend money and the coach's ability to judge talent and mold it into a cohesive unit, the team made it back to the playoffs in 1991.

The following season, Johnson's fourth year at the helm, the Cowboys won a franchise-record thirteen games in the regular season and reached the Super Bowl for an NFL-record sixth time. There, the Cowboys routed the Buffalo Bills 52-17 for their third championship. After that, fans came out in record numbers to see their heroes. The

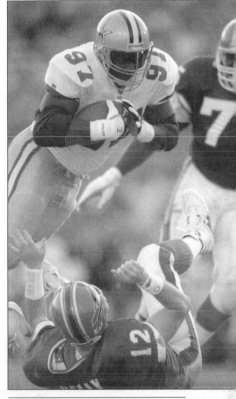

Defensive end Jimmie Jones dives for a touchdown, helping Dallas rout the Buffalo Bills in Super Bowl XXVII.

Cowboys sold out all of their regular season home games for the first time in eleven years and set a new team record for road attendance, playing before an average of more than 72,500 fans per game. The surge in attendance proved that Johnson's plan had been a success. The Cowboys had returned to their status as America's team.

Success followed upon success for Dallas. The following season they became just the third team in history to win a fourth Super Bowl, again defeating Buffalo, this time by a score of 30-13 in Super Bowl XXVIII. In spite of the club's success, however, the relationship between Jones and Johnson became strained due to a clash of wills between two men with giant egos. Johnson finally stepped down as coach in March 1994. To replace him, Jones hired former University of Oklahoma head coach, Barry Switzer.

The Cowboys won twelve games in Switzer's first year but were defeated by the 49ers in the NFC title game. They bounced back the next season to win yet another championship. With their 27-17 victory over the Pittsburgh Steelers in Super Bowl XXX, Dallas joined San Francisco as the only franchises to win five Super Bowls. Their eight appearances in the big game were three more than any other team, and winning three NFL titles in four years was an unprecedented accomplishment.

With a 27-17 victory over the Pittsburgh Steelers, Dallas tied San Francisco's record of five Super Bowl wins.

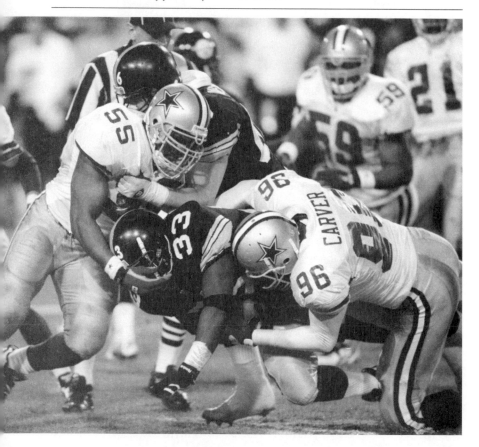

Tough Times

The years immediately following Dallas's victory in Super Bowl XXX have not been especially happy ones. The team's image was tarnished by several off-the-field incidents. These included a suspension for violation of the league's substance abuse policy by defensive tackle Leon Lett, and star receiver Michael Irvin's arrest for possession of illegal drugs in 1996, the "Year of Distraction." As Jerry Jones attempted to clean up the club's "bad boy" image, the head coach himself added to the problem. Just prior to the start of the 1997 season Barry Switzer was arrested for carrying a loaded, unlicensed .38-caliber revolver into Dallas–Fort Worth International Airport. For this, Jones assessed him a record seventy-five-thousand-dollar fine.

By the end of that season the Cowboys had dropped to a record of 6-10. Injuries, age, and free agency had taken their toll. Running back Emmitt Smith and defensive end Charles Haley were among the walking wounded, with Haley and tight end Jay Novacek eventually retiring. Defensive back (former Super Bowl Most Valuable Player) Larry Brown, kicker Chris Boniol, punter John Jett, and linebackers Godfrey Myles, Jim Schwantz, and Darrin Smith all left for other teams. Switzer was finally allowed to "resign" (rather than be fired), and was replaced by Chan Gailey for 1998. The team rebounded to 10-6 and became the first NFC East club ever to win all of its games within the division. It was quickly eliminated in the playoffs, however, losing in the first round to the Arizona Cardinals.

The next year Dallas broke even at 8-8, but managed to sneak into the playoffs as a wild card team. A loss to the Minnesota Vikings ended their season and was the death knell for Gailey. He was fired two days later.

A Time for Rebuilding

Although the decade ended on a sour note, Dallas was still considered the Team of the Nineties, winning three Super Bowls, six NFC Eastern Division championships, and making the playoffs eight times. *Financial World* magazine recognized the club as the most valuable in all of professional sports in 1993, 1994, and 1995.

Taking over the team for 2000, in his first season as an NFL head coach (a trait common to each of the five men who have coached

Dallas), was Cowboys defensive coordinator Dave Campo. Campo quickly learned he had his work cut out for him. The Cowboys won just five games in 2000 against eleven losses.

Campo will be given the opportunity to turn the team around, but he faces a stiff challenge. The Cowboys no longer have the offensive triumvirate of wide receiver Michael Irvin, quarterback Troy Aikman, and running back Emmitt Smith on which to fall back (first round draft picks in 1988, 1989, and 1990, respectively). Irvin retired following the 1999 season, Aikman was released in March 2001, and years of wear and tear have begun to show on Smith.

One cannot count the Cowboys out, however, since they have come from even farther back in the past. Team owner Jones, eager to see the team regain its once-lofty status, remains optimistic, confident of his ability to rebuild a winning team. It will surely be only a matter of time until "America's Team" once again returns to its position atop the National Football League.

Since coming into existence as a collection of players no one wanted, the Dallas Cowboys have become one of the National Football League's most popular teams by fielding Hall of Fame players and giving fans an exciting brand of football. Such a combination assures their legacy as one of pro football's greatest teams.

CHAPTER 2

Tom Landry

Tom Landry was the Dallas Cowboys. He took over an expansion team and helped establish it as one of the most famous—and most successful—franchises in American sports. As a player he was an All-Pro; as a coach he was a Hall of Famer. He introduced many innovations that are staples of the modern professional game. More important, he was an example and inspiration to others, performing his job with the highest degree of integrity and character. As former Miami Dolphins coach Don Shula said, "The National Football League is what it is today because of people like him, not only in terms of the job he did in coaching, but also the example he set for fair play."[7] No greater legacy can be left by any man.

"Terrific Tommy" Landry

Thomas Wade Landry was born on September 11, 1924, in Mission, Texas, a small town in the Rio Grande Valley near the Mexican border. He was the third child born to Ray and Ruth Landry. Older brother Robert, older sister Ruth, and younger brother Jack completed the family. Tom's dad was an automobile mechanic and volunteer fireman known to everyone in Mission. He and his wife imparted strong Christian values to their children as well as an appreciation for hard work.

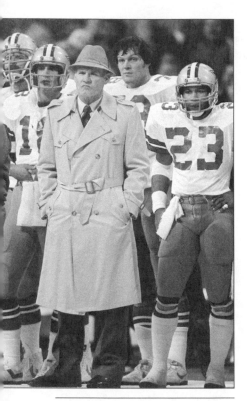

Coach Tom Landry introduced innovations that are staples of modern football.

As a youngster Tom was shy and self-conscious, in part because of a speech impediment. He found an outlet in sports, developing his skills on the Texas sandlots. When he entered Mission High School he had enough confidence in himself to go out for the junior varsity football team. On the very first day of practice coach Bob Martin held up a football and announced, "I need a smart, tough kid who will take this ball and initiate every play for our team."[8] Landry immediately volunteered and became the team's center.

Landry moved up to the varsity team as a junior and was converted to quarterback. At this position he had immediate success, leading the Eagles to a 6-4 record. In Landry's senior year the team went undefeated as "Terrific Tommy" led the squad to a regional championship. The only touchdown scored against Mission that season came on a disputed call. Playing at defensive back against Donna, a rival school, Landry broke up a pass in the end zone but was called for interference. The referee mistakenly awarded Donna a touchdown instead of giving them the ball on the 1-yard line. Mission won the game 12-7, and the official later apologized for missing the call.

In each of his two varsity seasons Landry received All-South Texas honors. He decided to continue his career at the University of Texas, where he was awarded a football scholarship. During his freshman year he received news that his older brother Robert—who had enlisted in the service following the Japanese attack on Pearl Harbor the previous December—was missing in action. His sibling's death was extremely hard for the eighteen-year-old to deal with. However, that November he enlisted in the army reserves. He eventually became a B-17 bomber pilot and flew thirty combat missions in Europe, surviving one crash landing in Belgium after a bombing run in Czechoslovakia.

When the war ended, Landry returned to the University of Texas. With future Hall of Famer Bobby Layne now ahead of him at quarterback, Landry was switched to defensive back and running back. "Giving up his quarterback job to play defensive back was a setback to him," said former teammate Dick Harris. "But Tom was such a competitor, it was clear the coaches were going to find a way to get him on the field, no matter the position."[9] As a defensive back Landry became known for his sure tackling and helped the team to a 10-1 record in 1947.

The next year Landry was named one of the team's captains. Although the Longhorns compiled a disappointing 6-3-1 record, they were invited to the Orange Bowl where Landry had the best game of his college career. Subbing at fullback for an injured teammate, he ran for 117 yards to lead Texas to an upset victory over Georgia.

Next Stop, the Pros

As Landry walked off the field after the Orange Bowl game he was approached by an assistant coach from the New York Yankees professional football team of the All America Football Conference (AAFC). The coach offered him a contract on the spot. However, Landry had never intended to play professional football. He planned to settle down and marry his college sweetheart, Alicia Wiggs. The money the Yankees were offering—six thousand dollars, including a five-hundred-dollar bonus—changed his mind. He signed that night, knowing he could now afford to marry Alicia. They married on January 28, 1949.

Tom played just one season with the Yankees before the team—and the league—folded. That one season, however, provided him with a very important lesson. It came in a game against the league-champion Cleveland Browns.

Landry started the contest when an injury befell one of the Yankees' starting defensive backs. Cleveland's immortal coach Paul Brown had his quarterback, Otto Graham, take advantage of the rookie every chance he had. Cleveland's Mac Speedie, the receiver Landry was to cover, set league single-game records for receptions

(11) and yards receiving (228). Although it was the most embarrassing performance of Landry's career as an athlete, it taught him something very important. "I realized my own limitations," he later recalled. "I conceded that it was impossible to succeed solely on skill, on emotion, or even on determination. Any success I ever attained would require the utmost in preparation and knowledge."[10]

After the AAFC's demise, Landry signed with the New York Giants of the National Football League. He starred for the team as a defensive halfback and punter over the next several seasons. Together with teammate Emlen Tunnell, Landry became one of the cornerstones of the Giants' famous "Umbrella Defense," so called

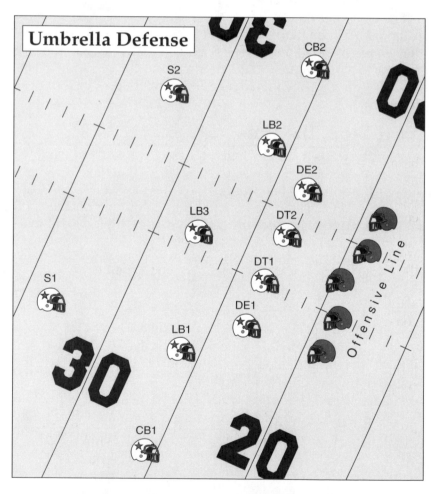

Head coach Jim Lee Howell, center, stands with Tom Landry, second from left, Vince Lombardi, far right, and other New York Giants assistants.

because the four defensive backs were arranged in an umbrella-like shape. The defense was especially effective in preventing fast receivers from coming out of the backfield since the two defensive ends would drop back, opening up the "umbrella" even more.

Despite his experience at quarterback in college, Landry had always been especially fascinated with defense. "I felt defense was the most challenging part of the game," he would recall. "The offense has its plays diagramed for it and knows ahead of time exactly what it has to do. On the other hand, the defense must constantly anticipate and react."[11]

This infatuation with defense led him to accept a full-time job as defensive coordinator with the Giants when he retired following the 1955 season (after being a player-coach for two years). With Landry in charge of the defense and Vince Lombardi handling the offense, head coach Jim Lee Howell's 1956 Giants were a potent force. They finished the season with an 8-3-1 record and played the Chicago Bears for the NFL championship on December 30. The game was played in front of fifty-six thousand fans on a frozen field in New York. Wearing basketball shoes to give them better traction, the Giants jumped out to an early lead and eventually won by a score of 47-7. It was the team's first championship since 1938. Howell was quick to credit his assistants for their contributions to the team's success. "With Lombardi coaching the offense, and Landry coaching the defense," he said, "all I ever have to do is keep the balls pumped up and enforce curfew."[12]

Among Landry's innovations as a coach was a new defensive alignment called the 4-3. Essentially, this created the middle linebacker position. This revolutionary idea of moving one of the five defensive linemen back several feet behind the line of scrimmage was eventually adopted by every NFL team. His success with New York led head coach Howell to call him "the greatest football coach in the game today."[13]

The Birth of a New Team

Others were also aware of Landry's defensive expertise. Clint Murchison Jr. and Tex Schramm contacted him about coaching a new expansion franchise on which they were bidding. On December 27, 1959—more than a month before the franchise was even awarded—they signed him to a five-year contract with an annual salary of $34,000.

The Dallas Cowboys, as the new team was called, could not take part in the college draft that first year since it was held prior to their acceptance into the league. Their roster was stocked with available players from other National Football League teams in an expansion pool. With this collection of castoffs the Cowboys entered the NFL in 1960.

The results were not pretty. In the franchise's first regular season game the Cowboys lost to the Pittsburgh Steelers, 35-28. With the exception of a 31-31 tie with the Giants in the next-to-last week of the season, Dallas lost all the other games they played that year.

However, by 1962, Landry had begun to work his magic. Despite winning just five games, the Cowboys scored 393 points to finish second in the league, mainly as a result of his offensive innovations. One innovation included having players shift position one or more times before the ball was snapped. "I realized that I couldn't beat anyone with my personnel," he explained. "So I had to do it with the motion and formations and gadget plays, the kind of stuff that bothered me most when I was a defensive coach."[14]

The early years were tough on Landry and the Cowboys. The coach expected his players to give their best effort, but knew realistically that they were destined to struggle since this was basically a team of castoffs. Some players resented what they considered unreasonable expectations. Murchison and Schramm, however, endorsed Landry completely. In order to show their support they signed him to an unprecedented ten-year contract extension in February 1964. At the time the team's overall record for the first four years of its existence was 13-38-3.

Up until then Landry's plan had been to coach for a few years, then retire and go into business. The new contract made him rethink his priorities. "I reevaluated what my life purpose was," he said. "Being in God's plan, I felt like it was a calling for me to coach."[15] The contract extension ensured that he would have a chance to see the offensive seeds he had planted grow to fruition.

Success at Last

With Landry as coach the Cowboys posted their first winning season in 1966, taking the Eastern Conference crown. For his efforts Landry was named NFL Coach of the Year. Remarkably, the team would not have another losing season for twenty years.

While the 1966 season marked the start of Dallas's run as one of the top teams in the league, it also began a period of frustration for Landry and his players. Although he guided them into the postseason year after year, they could not take the final step to a championship. In both 1966 and 1967 they lost to the Green Bay Packers in the NFL championship game. The next two years they fell to the Cleveland Browns in the Eastern Conference title game. The Cowboys made it all the way to the Super Bowl in 1970, but lost there to the Baltimore Colts, 16-13.

One Dallas sportswriter sarcastically referred to them as "Next Year's Champions," but Landry refused to let the players feel sorry for themselves. Instead, he encouraged them to build upon the losses. "The world doesn't stop when you lose," he explained. "You must think about the good things that happened to you. You must look ahead."[16] And look ahead is exactly what they did.

In 1971 the Cowboys at long last shed their label as losers. They compiled an 11-3 record during the regular season, then advanced through the playoffs to the Super Bowl where they took on the

"Stoneface" Landry smiles as he is carried off the field after defeating the Miami Dolphins in Super Bowl VI.

Miami Dolphins. With Landry calling the shots, the Cowboys pounded Miami, 24-3, to win Super Bowl VI and bring the championship to Dallas. The always-serious, unemotional coach—known as "Stoneface" to some of the Cowboys—was carried off the field on his players' shoulders. "I don't think I'm really conscious of my feelings yet," he said later. "This is certainly my biggest thrill."[17]

This period also saw Landry institute several new ideas. The concept of having specialty coaches for strength and speed programs was Landry's and was instituted in the early 1970s. He was also the first to have a quality-control coach, who helped the club by analyzing game films of future opponents and charting their offensive and defensive tendencies. These innovations gave the

Cowboys an edge over other teams and helped them maintain their position among the league's top teams.

The thrills would keep coming for the rest of the decade. The Cowboys won another Super Bowl in 1977, and lost two others in 1975 and 1978. For the decade, they failed to win at least ten games only once (1974). Their three Super Bowl losses were each by four points or less—16-13 to Baltimore (1970 season), 21-17 to Pittsburgh (1975), and 35-31 to Pittsburgh (1978).

Dallas's string of successes and near-misses helped establish it as America's Team. Its players included stars such as quarterback Roger Staubach; defensive tackle Randy White; linebacker Hollywood Henderson; and running back Duane Thomas. All were

Tossing his arms in the air, Landry shows his disgust after losing his third Super Bowl in ten years.

molded into a winning combination by Landry, their unflappable leader. The coach, however, did not believe he had any magical formula for success. "Leadership," he said, "is a matter of having people look at you and gain confidence, seeing how you react. If you're in control, they're in control." [18]

The Decline

The 1980s began with a twelve-win season for Dallas. The team twice came up short of a title, losing in the NFC title game both years. The strike-shortened season of 1982 saw them compile a 6-3 mark, followed by another twelve wins in 1983. In 1984 the club finished at 9-7 and failed to make the playoffs for the first time since 1974. After a 10-6 record in 1985, Dallas finished at 7-9 the next year, snapping its amazing streak of twenty consecutive winning seasons.

Landry seriously began to consider retirement. Many fans were less kind, calling for his firing. At least one went even further. During a December loss to the Rams, Landry received a death threat. He left the field and returned wearing a bulletproof vest.

In 1987, Landry was offered a three-year extension to give him a chance to turn the team's fortunes around. Later that year, however, he came in for criticism from the front office. "If the teacher doesn't teach," said general manager Tex Schramm, "the student doesn't learn." [19] It appeared that age and the refusal of some modern players to submit to his strict disciplinary methods might finally be catching up to Landry.

The next season the team's record dropped to 3-13, Dallas's worst mark since its very first year. More and more people called for Landry's job. The coach, however, refused to back down. In mid-February of 1989, Landry announced his intentions of coaching into the 1990s and returning the team to its winning ways. Unfortunately, this was not to be the case.

The End of an Era

Arkansas oilman Jerry Jones bought the Cowboys on February 25, 1989. On the same day, he announced that Landry had been fired. Jones replaced him with his former college friend and teammate at the University of Arkansas, Jimmy Johnson.

Landry accepted the decision but was upset at the way it was handled. He said good-bye to his players two days later as words of praise poured in from all quarters. "There are relatively few coaches whose careers compare with Tom," said NFL commissioner Pete Rozelle. "No question he's a Hall of Famer, in my opinion. He's not only been an outstanding coach, but a tremendous role model for kids and our fans. He has contributed a tremendous amount to the league."[20] Shortly after the firing, the city of Dallas held a "Hats Off to Tom Landry Day." Approximately one hundred thousand people gathered at Texas Stadium for the celebration.

After his departure from coaching, Landry devoted much of his time to public service and charitable causes. "I don't ignore football," he said, "but I feel like I have a different calling in my life now."[21] His religion took on an even larger role in his life. He had been a member of the Fellowship of Christian Athletes since 1962 and had always tried to live his life according to his beliefs. "Coach Landry never really preached the Bible," said former player Mike Renfro. "He lived the right way."[22]

Landry was often the keynote speaker at rallies for the Billy Graham Crusades. In addition, he and his wife Alicia formed the Lisa Landry Childress Foundation in memory of their daughter, who died of liver cancer. The foundation, housed at Baylor Health Care Systems, works to increase public awareness of the need for organ donors.

Although Landry had been unceremoniously dismissed by the Cowboys, he was not forgotten by football. The year after he was fired he was inducted into the Pro Football Hall of Fame. In 1993 he was honored with induction into the Cowboys' Ring of Honor. He also remained involved in the Dallas sports scene by trying to lure sports events to the area as chairman of the Dallas International Sports Commission.

In 1999, Landry entered the hospital and was diagnosed with acute myelogenous leukemia. The disease, which occurs in only about five thousand people each year, causes an overproduction of white blood cells that inhibits the blood's ability to carry oxygen to all parts of the body. On February 12, 2000, after a nine-month battle with the disease, Landry passed away at the age of seventy-five.

Landry's Legacy

When Landry took the Dallas job he was just thirty-four years old. He spent twenty-nine years as the Cowboys' head man, tying

Green Bay's legendary Curly Lambeau for the record of most consecutive seasons as head coach of one team. Landry's teams won 270 games, third in league annals behind Don Shula and George Halas. The Cowboys won thirteen division titles over that span and played in five Super Bowls, winning two and losing the others by a total of eleven points.

Landry led the Cowboys to thirteen division titles and five Super Bowls in his twenty-nine years as head coach.

Landry, the man who impassively walked the sidelines in his trademark fedora, was responsible for numerous innovations. In addition to being one of the architects of the 4-3 defense while with the Giants, he helped devise the Cowboys' famed multiple-set offense, the most complex offensive system to date. He later revamped the 4-3 as the Flex defense. In this formation two of the linemen line up a couple steps behind the others, allowing them more lateral movement. This alignment became part of Dallas's famous Doomsday Defense which helped carry the Cowboys to their Super Bowl successes.

Perhaps Landry's greatest impact, however, was in his approach to the game. His preparation and fanatical attention to detail gave his players the best possible chance for success. "The greatest thing Coach Landry did," said former player and NFL coach Dan Reeves, "is that he had us prepared for everything an opponent might do. We were rarely surprised."[23]

Landry's legacy has continued through the work of the coaches he helped produce, including Dan Reeves and Mike Ditka. Even Jerry Jones, the man who fired him, acknowledged his stature. "We will never be able to measure the complete significance of coach Landry's contributions to the Dallas Cowboys," he said. "Simply stated, he is the single most important figure in the history of this franchise."[24]

CHAPTER 3

Bob Lilly

In Dallas Cowboys' history, Bob Lilly is a man of many firsts. He was the team's first-ever draft choice in 1961, the first player named to the Cowboys' Ring of Honor (in 1975), and the first Cowboy inducted into the Pro Football Hall of Fame (in 1980). He was the foundation of the team's great defensive units of the late sixties and early seventies, known as the Doomsday Defense. His strength and quickness helped make him arguably the most dominant defensive lineman of his day. In the words of coach Tom Landry, "A man like this comes along once in a generation. Nobody was better than Lilly." [25]

A Texan Through and Through

Robert Lewis Lilly was born in Olney, Texas, on July 26, 1939. He grew up in the small town of Throckmorton, where his dad owned a farm.

Ever since the first grade Bob was bigger and stronger than the other kids his age. As he recalled, "We used to have wars where you put a guy on your shoulder, and you fought each other, and I was always the horse, with a guy sitting on my shoulder." [26] Some of the kids made fun of him because of his size, teasing him and then running away. When he got fast enough to catch them, however, the teasing stopped.

Like most boys in Texas, young Bob grew up with football. His father had broken a bone in his leg when he was a boy and it had not been properly set. Because of this he was never able to participate in sports. He did, however, introduce his son to football and became his biggest fan. Mr. Lilly's hero had been Washington Redskins' quarterback Sammy Baugh, who was raised just thirty miles from Throckmorton and had played his college ball at Texas Christian University (TCU). When Bob was just eight or nine years old, his dad took him to see the Oil Bowl classic in Wichita Falls. "I used to dream of being good enough to be in the Oil Bowl," recalled Lilly, "even to just make the team."[27]

By the time Bob was in the eighth grade he was already six-feet three-inches tall and weighed 155 pounds. His height made him a

natural for basketball and he favored that sport until he began to put on weight. By his sophomore year in high school he was 195 pounds; by his senior year he was up to 230.

Bob played basketball and football for tiny Throckmorton High School until his senior season. That year a severe seven-year drought in West Texas finally took its toll on the Lillys. With money hard to come by, the family moved north to Pendleton, Oregon, where they had relatives. As a senior at Pendleton High School, Bob starred in both basketball as a center and football as a defensive lineman. His size, speed, quickness, and agility could simply not be handled by opposing teams. He received numerous scholarship offers in both sports, including many from schools in the region.

Lilly's heart, however, was with TCU. When the drought ended in 1957, the family returned to Throckmorton. Bob accepted a scholarship to TCU and starred as a defensive lineman for the

Bob Lilly was the Cowboys first-ever draft choice, in 1961.

Horned Frogs for three seasons. While there he became known as the "Purple Cloud" because of the school's uniform colors. Tales of his incredible strength made him a local legend. One time a fellow student teased him by pointing to a Volkswagen parked nearby and saying, "If you're so strong, let's see you lift that VW onto the sidewalk."[28] Lilly examined the car carefully. He walked around and lifted the rear end onto the sidewalk, then did the same to the front end. He would later laugh at how the tale grew with each retelling. "It got so that some people were saying that I put the car up on the library steps," he said.[29]

Texas Christian University had good but not great sports teams during that period. Nevertheless, in his senior year of 1960, Lilly was a unanimous all-American and caught the eye of many pro scouts. Having grown up in Texas, Lilly knew he wanted to play there as a pro. The Cowboys had just entered the National Football League in 1960, and with fellow Texan Tom Landry as the team's head coach, it was natural for Lilly to prefer Dallas.

The American Football League had also just begun play. Bob let it be known that the Dallas Texans of the new league were his second choice after the Cowboys. With Lilly having announced his desire to play only for a Texas-based team, most NFL clubs were scared off, not willing to take a chance on drafting the giant defensive tackle and then not being able to sign him to a contract.

Knowing that Lilly wanted to play for Dallas, the Cowboys went about moving up in their drafting position to improve their chances of selecting him. They had traded their first-round pick to Washington in the 1960 deal that brought quarterback Eddie LeBaron to Dallas. On draft day, however, they acquired Cleveland's top pick, the thirteenth overall selection of the draft, in exchange for their own top two choices in 1962. With that pick the Cowboys selected Bob Lilly.

The Foundation of a Champion

In Lilly's first two years with the Cowboys he played left defensive end in the team's 4-3 defensive alignment (four linemen at the line of scrimmage and three linebackers behind them). He struggled, since ends have to run longer distances to chase down ball-carriers and quarterbacks. Lilly had exceptional quickness but not good long-range speed. In addition, he had "reacted" to plays as a

Lilly (74) tackles quarterback Y. A. Tittle moments after he releases a pass for a touchdown.

defensive tackle in college. Now he had to learn how to "read" his opponent to get an idea of the type of play being called. His inexperience showed as he struggled those first two seasons. The Cowboys did likewise, posting records of 4-9-1 in 1961 and 5-8-1 in 1962.

The Dallas clubs of those early years had many older players who had been with other teams that used different offensive and defensive systems. They were set in their ways and did not necessarily agree with Landry's way of doing things. Players complained and blamed each other when things went wrong. Unhappy Cowboys were gradually weeded out, but the atmosphere on the team added to Lilly's woes. "That was a humbling experience," said Lilly, "playing defensive end in pro football without ever having played it before. I just didn't fit. Those two years I hated football. I could not stand being out there at the end. I wanted to be in the middle of things."[30]

Despite having problems at his new position, Lilly was still making an impact on the league. He led the Cowboys in sacks both seasons, and earned the respect of opposing players. In one game against the Cleveland Browns in his rookie year, Lilly collided head-on with the Browns' all-time great runner Jim Brown. The powerful Brown was hit with such force, he staggered away after getting up and headed for the Cowboys' defensive huddle rather than the Browns' offensive one.

In his third year in the league, the six-foot five-inch, 260-pound Lilly finally got his wish. He was shifted from left defensive end to his natural position of right defensive tackle and blossomed into a star. In this inside position he could better take advantage of his strength and quickness. In describing that quickness, Landry said, "Lilly always broke through his first block. Always. And sometimes through second and third blocks. There is no one man in football who can contain Lilly."[31]

The Flex Defense

In 1964 the Cowboys began to experiment with Landry's Flex defense. In this scheme six of the front seven defensive players were responsible for covering one gap (opening between two linemen) each. This had the effect of taking away a player's natural instincts of pursuit. Instead of going after a particular man, defensive linemen were expected to control their individual areas, waiting for the ball to come to them.

The next year the Cowboys went to the Flex more and more, with Lilly in the key position. "They designed the Flex defense *for* him," said teammate Maury Youmans.[32] Former Cowboys' assistant coach Dick Nolan explained, "Lilly wasn't a sprinter of any kind. He wasn't a great 40-yard guy. But he was so quick for five or ten yards, and brother, once he got his hands on you, he was so strong, too, you couldn't get away. And he'd throw you any way he wanted to."[33] With the success of the Flex defense in 1965, the Cowboys won as many games as they lost for the first time in their history.

Although the Cowboys continued to improve over the ensuing years, they failed to win a championship. In the NFL championship game in 1966 the Green Bay Packers took an early lead over Dallas, but the Cowboys fought back valiantly. The Packers

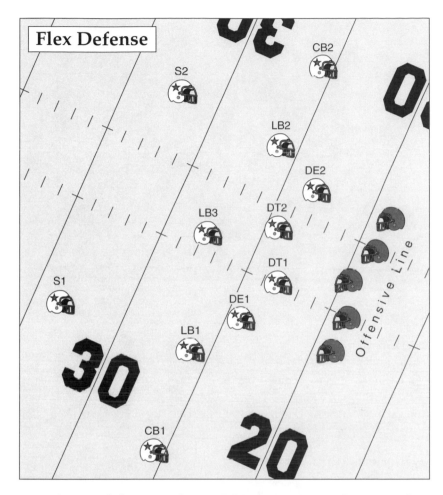

scored a touchdown with just 5:20 remaining in the game, but Lilly blocked Don Chandler's extra point attempt to keep the Cowboys within range at 34-20. Inspired by the blocked kick, Dallas immediately came back to score on a sixty-eight-yard pass play, then got the ball back after Green Bay was forced to punt. The Cowboys advanced all the way to the Green Bay 2-yard line, but a fourth-down pass was intercepted, sealing the Packers' win.

In 1967, Dallas won its division for the second year in a row. The team was to meet the Cleveland Browns for the right to play in the NFL championship game. Four days before the game, however, tragedy struck. Lilly's seven-week-old daughter Carmen died suddenly in her crib. Lilly was devastated. His teammates

The Cowboys championship run ended with a loss to the Green Bay Packers in the famous "Ice Bowl" game.

shared his grief and gave him their support. As he later recounted, "Practicing was my only way of getting relief, and I wouldn't have missed that game for anything. But it was very sad. It was one of those times. . . . I just went out there against Cleveland and played as hard as I could."[34]

Playing like a man possessed, Lilly had one of the greatest games of his career. He sacked Cleveland quarterback Frank Ryan three times and knocked down two passes. The Cowboys ran over the Browns, defeating them by a score of 52-14 before more than seventy thousand screaming fans. It was the first playoff win in the team's history.

Dallas's run at a championship took them to Green Bay, Wisconsin, the next week, where the club played the Green Bay Packers in the famous Ice Bowl game. Shortly after waking up that morning, Lilly threw a cup of water against the window of his hotel room. The water froze on the glass. The game was played in minus-thirteen-degree temperatures, the coldest December 31 in Green Bay history. Lilly gave a solid performance in a thrilling contest that the Packers won, 21-17, to end the Cowboys' bid for a championship.

By 1970 the Cowboys were ready to make another run for the Super Bowl. After winning their division, they beat the Detroit Lions and San Francisco 49ers to advance to Super Bowl V against the Baltimore Colts. The Cowboys lost a 16-13 heartbreaker to the underdog Colts, who scored the winning points on a field goal with just five seconds remaining in the game. The frustration of the loss was seen in Lilly's reaction. "After the ball went through the uprights and we lost," recounted teammate Lee Roy Jordan, "Bob Lilly threw his helmet about three hundred feet in the air, and when it hit the ground, it splattered into pieces. Pieces just flew everywhere, I can't believe he threw it that high in the air."[35]

Dallas returned to the big game in 1971. Their opponent in Super Bowl VI was Miami. The Cowboys completely dominated the Dolphins before more than eighty-one thousand people at Tulane Stadium in New Orleans. They advanced to a 3-0 lead that they never relinquished, winning by a final score of 24-3. One of the most memorable plays of the game came when Lilly shot through the Miami offensive line and chased after quarterback Bob Griese. He eventually caught him for a twenty-nine-yard loss, the biggest loss on a sack in Super Bowl history. "When they mention that football game," said Cowboys' general manager Tex Schramm, "they don't mention any of the touchdowns or any of the other plays, they always mention Bob Lilly chasing down Bob Griese."[36]

The Super Bowl victory was the highlight of Lilly's pro career. "It's the ultimate feeling a person can have," he said.[37] While attending Texas Christian University, Lilly had set three goals in his life. The first—to

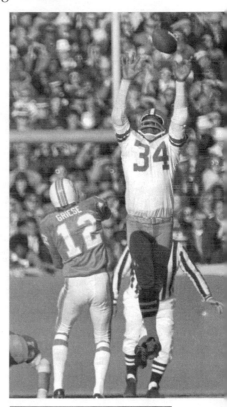

A Dallas defender leaps high in the air to block Bob Griese's end zone pass, helping the Cowboys win Super Bowl VI.

make all-American—he achieved in his senior season of 1960. The second—to make All-Pro—he attained for the first of seven times in 1964. The third—to win a Super Bowl—had now also been reached. Although Lilly would play three more seasons with the Cowboys, something was missing from his life. He needed a new goal. On July 20, 1975, a week before his thirty-sixth birthday, Bob Lilly announced his retirement from football.

A New Life

Shortly after his retirement, Lilly was awarded the Coors distributorship in Waco, Texas. He was determined to make the business a success. The distributorship was very lucrative, earning him much more money than his salary with the Cowboys ever had. The time he put into his business, however, put a strain on his marriage. Lilly felt his life getting out of control. "I realized how far I had strayed," he said, "not just because of the beer business, but just that ever since I had grown up, my life had gone a little off course."[38] He began attending church in an effort to give more meaning to his life.

While driving home to Dallas one night in 1982 an event occurred which made Lilly examine his life even further. A pickup truck had overturned and Lilly pulled over to see if he could help. He later recalled, "There were three boys inside, maybe 16 or 17 years old. They weren't hurt, just cut up pretty bad, but when I opened the door of that pickup, beer cans fell out all over me, and that's when I was convicted. It was like the Lord said, 'You know, Bob, what you see here is how you're using your fame, to sell beer to kids.'"[39] Soon afterward, he sold the profitable distributorship. "It was just the wrong business for me," he said. "I had a guilt feeling I could never get rid of."[40]

Much of Lilly's time is now spent indulging a hobby that he got involved in over forty years ago. While a senior at TCU in 1960 he was named to the Kodak All-American team. As part of the honor he was given a new camera and two hundred rolls of film. He began taking pictures and was soon hooked. He bought more and more equipment and built a darkroom in his home. Eventually he had a book of his work published—*Bob Lilly: Reflections*. He now specializes in landscape photography and sells many of his photos to magazines around the country. "I really enjoy it," he said. "It's very relaxing."[41]

The Honorable Bob Lilly

Lilly earned his time of relaxation. During his career, his play was so intense and consistently outstanding, he became known as "Mr. Cowboy." In fourteen seasons with the Cowboys he never missed a regular-season game, playing in a Dallas–record 196 consecutive contests. He played in two Super Bowls and eleven Pro Bowls in his career. His individual statistics include four touchdowns scored, one on an interception and three on recovered fumbles.

Praise came his way from teammates and opponents alike. Said Dallas quarterback Roger Staubach, "[Lilly's] the only player I ever remember who, when we'd watch our defensive films, other guys would oooh and aaah and talk about what he did."[42] Added former Washington Redskins head coach George Allen, "In my book, Bob Lilly was the greatest defensive tackle ever. We tried everything against him, but we couldn't confuse him or contain him. He seemed indestructible."[43]

Honors continued to come Lilly's way after his playing days were over. He was elected to the Pro Football Hall of Fame in 1980, and the College Football Hall of Fame the next year. In 1994 he was selected by the NFL to the league's 75th Anniversary All-Time team. Six years later the Hall of Fame Selection Committee named him to the All-Time NFL team.

Another honor is perhaps even more significant. Every year Dallas fans vote on a player to be given the Bob Lilly Award. It goes to the Cowboys player who displays the highest standards of leadership, sportsmanship, dedication, and achievement—the standards embodied by Robert Lewis Lilly.

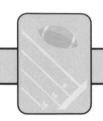

CHAPTER 4

Bob Hayes

In the 1964 Summer Olympics in Tokyo, Bob Hayes won two gold medals and the title of "World's Fastest Human." The next year he began terrifying NFL defensive backs with his speed from the Cowboys' wide receiver position.

Hayes is often credited with revolutionizing the game, by forcing teams to place more of an emphasis on speed. Prior to his arrival, defensive secondaries had used man-to-man coverage on receivers. Opposing teams quickly saw the futility of such a strategy against the fastest man in the league. As former Philadelphia Eagles defensive back Irv Cross explained, "If you've got a Bob Hayes who can run the 100 [yard dash] in 9.2, you'd better get a defensive back who can run the 100 in 9.2. Defensive backs got faster, more fast wide receivers came into the league, so, in a sense, Bob Hayes was the one who changed the direction of the game."[44]

Growing up in Jacksonville

Robert Lee Hayes was born in Jacksonville, Florida, on December 20, 1942. His mother, Mary Hayes, was a domestic who married a builder named Joseph Hayes. While Hayes was away fighting in World War II, his wife had an affair with a man named George

Sanders, resulting in the birth of their son, Robert. When Hayes returned from the war he accepted the boy as his own, although Bob was never legally adopted. Mary and Joe lived together on and off until Bob was eight years old. At that time they separated for good. Mary eventually married another man named John Robinson.

Credited with revolutionizing football, Bob Hayes forced teams to place more emphasis on speed.

George Sanders also entered the service during the war and was wounded in the South Pacific. When he returned to the States he opened a shoe shine parlor in East Jacksonville, but the store was just a front for his real business—an illegal numbers operation. Since he made good money illegally, Sanders did not place much of an emphasis on education. He rarely acknowledged Bob as his son and showed the boy little love or affection. Bob was closer to both Joe Hayes and John Robinson than he was to his real father.

Hayes grew up in a poor section of Jacksonville known as Hell's Hole. His mother had three other children, Nathaniel (who died as an infant), Ernest, and Lena. Mrs. Hayes always teased Bob about being a lazy baby who did not start walking until relatively late.

As a youngster, Bob was watched over by his brother Ernest, who was five years his senior. Ernest was an amateur boxer and Bob used to run with him. It was the future Cowboy's introduction to the activity.

During his youth Bob played Little League baseball and dreamed of becoming the next Willie Mays. At Matthew W. Gilbert High School he starred in baseball, football, basketball, and track. Football, however, soon became his passion. When it came time to decide on a college he opted for all-black Florida A&M, following in the footsteps of his idol, former Chicago Bears running back Willie Galimore.

Closing in on a World Record

Hayes starred for legendary coach Jake Gaither's squad as a running back and kickoff and punt returner. The team compiled a record of 27-3 in his three years on the varsity. Hayes's speed helped him post some impressive numbers. In one game against Bethune-Cookman College, Hayes ran for 121 yards on just eight carries—an average of over fifteen yards per carry. Another time, against Allen University, he gained 98 yards on just six rushing attempts (16.3 yards per carry). Hayes made the Southern Intercollegiate Athletic Conference (SIAC) all-star team in both his sophomore and junior years. In 1963 he was named the conference's outstanding athlete.

He first gained national recognition, however, for his running on coach Pete Griffin's track team. In his very first meet he won the hundred-yard dash in 9.4 seconds at the Florida A&M relays, equaling the record for college freshmen set by the immortal Jesse

Owens in 1934. As a sophomore in 1961 he tied the world record of 9.3 seconds for the hundred-yard dash. Before the record could be submitted for certification, however, it was eclipsed by Frank Budd of Villanova, who lowered the mark to 9.2 seconds.

Hayes himself ran a 9.2 in February 1962 but was denied a share of the record. The starter had used a .22-caliber pistol to begin the race instead of a .32-caliber. The latter gives off a more visible puff of smoke for the timers to start their watches by. Because of this technicality, Hayes's time was disallowed.

By the time he was a senior, Hayes had set new world marks in the 100-, 70-, and 60-yard dashes. It was all a prelude to his greatest moment of all. He became a household name around the world because of his performance in the 1964 Summer Olympics.

Olympic Glory

In September 1964, Hayes qualified for the Tokyo Olympics in the hundred-meter dash and entered the event as the favorite. He won in 10.06 seconds, tying both the world and Olympic marks. He also anchored the four-by-one-hundred-meter relay team to

Hayes pumps his hand in celebration after coming from behind to win the 4x100 relay at the 1964 Summer Olympics.

victory, running what the *Los Angeles Times* called "the most aston-
ishing sprint of all time."[45]

When Hayes took the baton—following Paul Drayton, Gerald
Ashworth, and Richard Stebbins—poor passing had put the
United States in fifth place, three meters behind France. Hayes
took off in one of the most awesome displays of sprinting ever
witnessed. After only thirty yards he had moved into the lead. He
crossed the finish line three meters ahead of second-place Poland,
leading his team to a new world record of 39.0 seconds. Although
there was disagreement as to his time, the slowest estimate was
8.9 seconds, with most being around an incredible 8.6. The relay
was the last competitive race of Hayes's career, and after the con-
clusion of the games he returned home to Florida.

Upon returning to college, Hayes had one year of football eligibility remaining. Hayes finished out the 1964 season at Florida
A&M. Upon the completion of the regular season, he played in the
North-South All-Star Game and was named the South squad's
most valuable player in his team's 37-30 loss. However, since 1963
was his fourth year at school, he had been available for the NFL
draft. On December 2, 1963, he was drafted by the Dallas Cowboys
in the seventh round. He was also drafted by the Denver Broncos
of the newly formed American Football League.

Hayes signed a one-hundred-thousand-dollar, three-year contract with the Cowboys on December 8, 1964. Former track stars
usually struggled in professional football, since track was generally
their first priority in college. Many believed Hayes would follow
suit. Tex Schramm, however, thought otherwise. "He's different
from the other track men who have attempted to play football in
that he has the natural moves and instincts of a football player,"
said the Dallas general manager.[46]

Welcome to the National Football League

Hayes's first game as a pro, however, caused some people to question his ability. Playing for the College All-Stars against the Cleveland Browns in August, he had trouble catching the ball,
prompting one observer to facetiously refer to him as the guy with
"9 flat speed and 12 flat hands."[47] The problem lay with quarterback Craig Morton. Morton threw the ball very hard, and during
practice his passes split open several of Hayes's fingers. The fin-

gers did not completely heal in time for the game and he had trouble holding on to the ball.

Despite his difficulties, Hayes reported to the Cowboys' training camp in Thousand Oaks, California, later that month. He came under the tutelage of Dallas receivers coach Howard "Red" Hickey. Hickey taught Hayes the fine points of the position, such as how to hold his hands in order to catch better and how to recognize defensive coverages. He spent hours of his own time honing Hayes's talents to bring his pass-catching skills up to his running abilities. In Hayes's words, "He's the one who really made me a professional football player."[48] Hickey, in turn, called Hayes the key to the team. "Bobby's arrival coincided with the beginning of the rise of the Cowboys," he said. "He became a star and he lifted the ball club. If ever any one man came in who started a team on the road to being exciting, he was the one."[49]

Nicknamed "Bullet Bob" because of his speed, Hayes worked diligently to improve and the results were striking. Midway through the first quarter of the season opener against the New York Giants, he caught a pass from quarterback Don Meredith for a 37-yard gain—his first official NFL catch. The first score of his career came late in the game on a 45-yard pass from Meredith. For his heroics, he was the first winner of the new Dallas Cowboys Player-of-the-Week Award.

Hayes continued to improve throughout the year. In a game against the Philadelphia Eagles he had eight receptions for 177 of Dallas's 250 passing yards. It was the third-highest yardage total in the club's history. He also scored a pair of touchdowns that day and, including punt and kickoff returns, accounted for a total of 253 yards. Red Hickey was effusive in his praise for his star pupil. "If nothing happens to [Hayes] physically," he said, "he'll have to be one of the all-time greats—just because there has never been another man with his possibilities. He has the most amazing speed in history, he has moves, he's tough, he's durable, he's teachable. What else can you ask?"[50]

Hayes finished the season with forty-six catches for 1,003 yards and twelve touchdowns, all Cowboy rookie records. He was only the second rookie in league history to surpass the thousand-yard mark, and his average of 21.8 yards per catch led the league. In addition, he finished third in punt returns (12.8 yards) and tied for sixth in kickoff returns (26.5). Hayes's play earned him the first of his three trips to the Pro Bowl, the league's postseason all-star game. In Rookie of the Year voting he finished second to Gale Sayers of the Chicago Bears. With Hayes as their spark, the Cowboys finished the year with a 7-7 record, the best of their brief existence.

Sprinting to the Top

Unlike many players, Hayes was not affected by the "sophomore jinx." The 1966 season was arguably the best of his professional career. He caught a total of sixty-four passes for 1,232 yards and thirteen touchdowns to earn his second consecutive Pro Bowl selection. In Dallas's 31-30 win over the Washington Redskins in November, Meredith and Hayes hooked up on a ninety-five-yard pass play, the longest in Cowboys' history. His 246 receiving yards on nine catches that day set another Dallas mark. When the St. Louis Cardinals lost their game in the next to last week of the season, it assured the Cowboys of winning the Eastern Division championship for the first time.

Dallas played the Green Bay Packers on New Year's Day for the NFL crown. The winner would represent the league in the first Super Bowl. Unfortunately for Dallas fans, the Cowboys lost to the Packers, 34-27. Hayes considered this the toughest loss of his career, putting much of the blame on himself. He caught only one pass that day, for a gain of one yard. On another play he foolishly tried to run a punt out of the end zone and was stopped at the 1-yard line. Finally, on Dallas's last play of the game, Hayes missed a block on a pass that resulted in a Green Bay interception.

Despite his troubles in the game against the Green Bay Packers, over the next couple of years Hayes continued to pile up sparkling numbers as the Cowboys took their place as one of the league's best teams. Despite his heroics, however, the Super Bowl managed to elude the Cowboys until 1970. That year Hayes began the season on the bench, a move he believed was racially motivated. He did not get his starting job back until the sixth week of the year, with Dallas struggling along with a 3-2 record. The Cowboys won six of their next eight games to stand at 9-4 going into the final week of the regular season.

On December 20—Hayes's twenty-eighth birthday—Dallas defeated the Houston Oilers, 52-10, to clinch the Eastern Division title.

Hayes had six receptions—including four for touchdowns—totaling 187 yards. The catches gave him 286 for his career, moving him past Frank Clarke into first place on the Dallas Cowboys all-time list.

In the playoffs, opposing teams concentrated on stopping Hayes, often giving him double- and triple-coverage. He did not have as many catches but still posed a breakaway threat. With

Hayes, a prolific receiver, surpassed Frank Clarke on Dallas's all-time list for most receptions, with 286.

The Baltimore Colts kicker leaps for joy after kicking the winning field goal in the final seconds of Super Bowl V.

quarterback Craig Morton having a poor game, Hayes again caught only one pass, for forty-one yards, in Super Bowl V against the Baltimore Colts. The Cowboys came up short in their quest for a championship as the Colts scored ten points in the fourth period to come from behind and win a mistake-filled game by a score of 16-13.

Champions at Last

Even though Hayes did not have a particularly outstanding post-season, he felt he was underpaid based on his performance since entering the league. He had played out his option in 1970 and became a free agent after the season. Although any team could have signed him, none made him an offer. The rule at the time allowed NFL commissioner Pete Rozelle to award what he considered fair compensation to any team that lost a player through free agency. A team that signed Hayes, therefore, would likely be forced to surrender their top receiver—or another star—to Dallas. No team was willing to take that chance. Hayes finally re-signed with the Cowboys, getting a five-year contract that, with incentives, was worth about eighty-five thousand dollars a year—a good salary, but less than he would have received had any team been truly free to sign him.

With his new contract in hand, Hayes proceeded to have another solid year in 1971, leading the league with a 24 yards-per-catch average for thirty-five receptions. The Cowboys again won the Eastern Division, with a record of 11-3. They began their post-season run with a 20-12 victory over the Minnesota Vikings on Christmas Day. Hayes gained just thirty-one yards on three catches, but one was for a touchdown in the third quarter.

Next, Dallas defeated the San Francisco 49ers in the NFC Championship game for the second year in a row. The contest was a defensive battle ending in a 14-3 score. The win put the Cowboys in the Super Bowl for the second time. Their opponent was the AFC-champion Miami Dolphins.

Bob Hayes carries the ball sixteen yards on an end-around play, putting Dallas in position to score in Super Bowl VI.

Super Bowl VI was played in Tulane Stadium in New Orleans, Louisiana. The Cowboys were favored to win. They advanced to a 3-0 lead in the first period on a field goal set up by an eighteen-yard pass to Hayes from Roger Staubach, who had taken over for Craig Morton as the starting quarterback in 1971. In the third quarter Hayes gained sixteen yards on an end sweep that put the ball on the Miami 6-yard line. The Cowboys went on to score a touchdown that gave them a 17-3 lead. When the final gun sounded, Dallas had a 24-3 win. The Cowboys had finally shed the title of "Next Year's Champions." With the victory, Hayes became the first person to win both an Olympic gold medal and a Super Bowl ring. It would be the crowning achievement of his football career.

A Downward Spiral

Over the next three years of his Cowboy career Hayes experienced a series of difficulties. Injuries, including a severely pulled

hamstring, began to take a toll on his body and significantly reduced his playing time. He caught a total of forty-four passes
from 1972 through 1974, just four going for touchdowns.

Hayes had also been an outspoken leader of the players' union.
In 1974 he made some critical comments about players who said
they would not support a strike if one was called by the NFL Players Association, suggesting they would be "marked men." This
caused friction between coach Tom Landry and Hayes, and resulted in dissension on the team. Hayes's role on the club was reduced even further as a result of his outspokenness, and trade
rumors began to circulate. They culminated on July 17, 1975,
when he was traded to the San Francisco 49ers in exchange for a
third-round draft choice.

Hayes lasted only four games with the 49ers before being released. He ended his career with 371 receptions for 7,414 yards and
71 touchdowns—numbers which should have made him a good
bet for election to the Pro Football Hall of Fame. Unfortunately, this
was not to be. Hayes lived a fast life off the field as well as on. His
troubles with the law following his retirement serve as a reminder
that athletes are still human beings, with human frailties, just like
everyone else.

*Ending his career with 371 receptions for 7,414 yards and 71 touchdowns,
Bob Hayes, statistically, was one of the best receivers in the NFL.*

In 1979, four years after leaving pro football, Hayes was arrested in Texas. He pleaded guilty to the possession and sale of cocaine, although he claimed that he never sold or used the drug. He was sentenced to five years in prison and served ten months before being paroled. Tex Schramm was one of those who believed that Hayes received a raw deal. "Bob had his problems," said Schramm, "but he was not a drug dealer. He was totally set up by an undercover cop trying to take down a big name."[51]

Depression set in following his release from prison. With his reputation and finances in ruins, Hayes looked to alcohol and drugs to help him escape from his problems. Unfortunately, they only added to them. He couldn't find a good job, his self-esteem had been destroyed, and most of his friends had turned their backs on him. His life had reached its lowest possible point.

The Road Back

Hayes entered rehabilitation in 1985 in order to try to get his life back in order. He was aided in his recovery by former teammate Roger Staubach. "He really needed some stability in his life," said Staubach. "He asked for some help and I tried to respond."[52]

Staubach gave Hayes a job with a commercial real estate company he owned. He helped him stick with his rehabilitation program and gave him the love and support he needed. Hayes returned to Florida A&M and earned his elementary education degree. He also gave talks around the country, speaking out against alcohol and drugs. "I speak to people," he said, "because I want everyone to know what I've been through. I point out the failures in my life."[53]

Because of his problems, Hayes has been denied election to the Pro Football Hall of Fame. Cowboys' owner Jerry Jones, however, has pushed for him to be chosen for the Cowboys' Ring of Honor. "All human beings can have excellence in one area and demons in another," said Jones. "I wouldn't do it if he'd committed crimes against other people, but Bob only hurt himself."[54]

Hayes faced yet another setback in early 2001. On March 6 he had his prostate removed after six weeks of radiation treatments for cancer. His friends are confident that he can overcome this most serious challenge of all. "He's a living legend," said former college roommate Al Denson. "If anyone can beat this thing, it's him."[55]

The "living legend" had an effect on the game that cannot be measured just in numbers. He showed that speed could play an integral—even critical—role in a team's offense. As he was always likely to go all the way for a touchdown whenever he touched the ball, he caused teams to change their ways of playing defense. Few players have ever had such a major impact on the way the game is played.

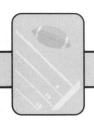

CHAPTER 5

Roger Staubach

In the 1970s, quarterback Roger Staubach symbolized the Dallas Cowboys. He became known as Captain America, leader of America's Team. Staubach led the Cowboys to four Super Bowls and eventually was enshrined in the Pro Football Hall of Fame. He earned a reputation as one of the greatest clutch performers in the history of the game, rallying his team to victory from the brink of defeat countless times in his eleven-year career. His pinpoint accuracy with passes and his ability to scramble out of danger and improvise when needed helped make him one of the most successful quarterbacks in NFL history.

Staubach won every honor imaginable on the field of play. Even more important, however, was his character. He was a courageous, loyal, hard worker, devoted to his family and his beliefs. As coach Tom Landry once said, "If there is a Hall of Fame for people, then they better save a spot there for him, too."[56]

The All-American Boy

Roger Thomas Staubach, an only child, was born to Robert and Betty Staubach of Cincinnati, Ohio, on February 5, 1942. His father was sales manager for a shoe manufacturer's agent and his mother was a homemaker.

Roger Staubach, known as Captain America, leader of America's Team, guided the Cowboys to four Super Bowls, becoming a Hall of Famer.

Roger's parents were devout Catholics and he was raised with a strong grounding in the faith. He went to St. John's Parochial School in Deer Park, a suburb of Cincinnati. There, the nuns had a great influence on him, teaching him Christian values and a disciplined work ethic.

Like every child, Roger had many interests. His mother encouraged him to play the piano, but he was more interested in sports. As Mrs. Staubach once recalled, "The music teacher said she couldn't compete with the kids on the porch."[57] From the age of seven Roger was involved in organized sports. He played on a baseball team co-managed by his father and on the football team at St. John's when he was in the seventh grade.

The self-discipline he learned from the nuns served him well when he entered the all-boys Purcell High School in Cincinnati. He was able to maintain a B-plus average while starring in football, basketball, and baseball. He was also elected president of his class as a senior.

Roger was good enough in basketball to make the all-city team. In baseball he competed in several summer leagues, where his opponents included future major leaguers Pete Rose and Eddie Brinkman. Football, however, was his main love. Staubach played tight end and defensive back as a freshman, then some quarterback during his sophomore year. A broken hand forced him back to defense as a junior, so his senior year was his first full season leading the team. Despite having a strong arm, Roger threw only five or six times a game. He also learned to scramble (run around behind the line of scrimmage to avoid would-be tacklers after pass protection has broken down), a skill that would be one of his trademarks in later years, in coach Jim McCarthy's T-formation offense.

The Midshipman

When it came time to choose a college, Roger had many options. He was offered athletic scholarships by twenty-five schools. He was interested in both Notre Dame and Purdue, but eventually decided on the United States Naval Academy at Annapolis, Maryland. Unfortunately, his SAT score in English was just shy of the mark required for entrance. The navy funded his education for a year at New Mexico Military Academy, where he gained additional experience as a quarterback.

In Staubach's sophomore year at Annapolis (1962), he began the season as coach Wayne Hardin's fifth-ranked quarterback. Injuries and poor performances by the players ahead of him, however, soon gave him a chance to play. In the fourth game of the year he entered a scoreless contest against Cornell. He ran for two touchdowns, threw for one, and led his team to a 41-0 win. His performance the rest of the season earned him the Thompson Trophy as the naval academy's top athlete. He would win the award in each of his three varsity seasons, the only player ever to do so.

As a junior in 1963, Staubach led Navy to a 9-1 record and a number two ranking in the nation. He completed 66.5 percent of his passes (107 of 161) to lead the nation for the second consecutive year. Roger was also the team's second-leading rusher, with 418 yards gained on the ground. In the postseason Cotton Bowl, Navy lost to top-ranked Texas, but Staubach set a Cotton Bowl record by completing 21 of 31 passes for 228 yards. For his performance that season he won the Heisman Trophy as the nation's outstanding college player, becoming just the fourth junior in history to be so honored. "I played well, but my teammates were really the instrumental part of my success," said Roger. "In fact, I promised that I'd cut it up in pieces and give it to them. They're still waiting for that, by the way." [58]

Navy Duty

Because he had spent a year in junior college, Staubach was eligible for the National Football League draft in 1964. He was picked by the Cowboys in the tenth round. He was not chosen sooner because teams knew he had a commitment to four years of military service following his graduation. Most thought he would never play in the NFL. Staubach was also drafted by the Kansas City Chiefs of the American Football League, but after finishing out an injury-plagued senior season, he signed a Dallas contract that called for a ten-thousand-dollar bonus and five hundred dollars a month for the time he remained in the navy.

When it came time to select his service options, Staubach volunteered for duty in Vietnam, where he was stationed for a year. After returning to the States he ran the supply arm of the Pensacola naval base in Florida. Roger attended the Cowboys training camp in 1968 while on leave, then joined the team the following year at the age of twenty-seven.

A Quarterback Controversy

When Staubach joined Dallas in 1969, Craig Morton was the starting quarterback. Roger's diligent work ethic, however, soon made

Scrambling out of danger, Staubach had an uncanny ability to improvise when plays broke down.

him a favorite of coach Tom Landry. He would remain on the practice field for hours, working on the parts of his game that needed improvement. Landry was not thrilled, however, with his penchant for scrambling when the pocket [blocking] around him broke down. The offense had confidence in the system that had won in the past and generally preferred Morton.

When an injury sidelined Morton, Staubach started in the opening game of the year against the St. Louis Cardinals. The first touchdown of his career came on a sixty-yard pass to Lance Rentzel. Staubach contributed to Dallas's 24-3 victory by displaying an accurate arm and an ability to scramble out of danger and improvise when plays broke down.

Morton soon returned to action and was leading the league in passing when he hurt his shoulder. Playing the rest of the year at less than full strength, he still led Dallas to an 11-2-1 record. A loss to the Cleveland Browns in the playoffs, however, ended the Cowboys' year on a disappointing note.

The injured shoulder continued to plague Morton in 1970, but he managed to lead the team to Super Bowl V, where the Cowboys lost to the Baltimore Colts, 16-13. On the plane flight back to Dallas after the game, Staubach wondered about his future with the team. If he couldn't play when Morton was hurting, Roger decided it was time to ask to be traded. Just then, Landry sat down next to him and told him the words he wanted to hear. "You will get your opportunity to be a starting quarterback this coming season," said the coach. [59]

At the Controls

The next year, with Morton having recovered from his shoulder woes, Landry announced that the Cowboys would have two starting quarterbacks for the 1971 season. After six games of the regular season he went even further, saying that Morton and Staubach would alternate plays. That experiment resulted in a 23-19 loss to the Chicago Bears, which dropped Dallas's record to 4-3.

The following week Landry told Staubach the starting job was his for the rest of the season. "I won't let you down, Coach," promised Roger. [60] He proceeded to make good on that promise. In his first start he led Dallas to a thrilling 16-13 victory over the St. Louis Cardinals. He went undefeated over the final seven games of the regular season, guiding the Cowboys to the Eastern Division championship. Roger completed 59.7 percent of his passes, including fifteen for touchdowns, and ran for 343 yards (an average of 8.4 yards per carry).

Despite the team's success, Staubach and Landry clashed over the coach's insistence on calling all the plays from the bench. Many times a play would be sent in from the sidelines and Staubach would change it at the line of scrimmage. "It wasn't to the point where they got angry," recalled wide receiver Margene Adkins, "where Staubach wanted to run the team and Tom Landry wanted to. It was just a little problem there." [61]

Staubach's magic continued through the playoffs. The Cowboys defeated the Minnesota Vikings in the divisional playoff, then bested the San Francisco 49ers in the NFC Championship game. On January 16, 1972, they met the Miami Dolphins in Super Bowl VI in New Orleans.

Staubach completed his unbeaten streak as the starting quarterback by leading the team to a 24-3 win over the Dolphins. He

completed twelve of nineteen passes for 119 yards and two touchdowns. For his efforts he was named the game's most valuable
player. Many, however, felt that running back Duane Thomas
should have won the award. Thomas was a controversial player
who had a poor relationship with the media. Roger modestly said,
"Duane would have gotten the MVP if he would have talked to
the press. . . . That's the only reason he didn't get the award."[62]

*Staubach prepares to throw the ball in his first start of the 1971 season,
against the St. Louis Cardinals.*

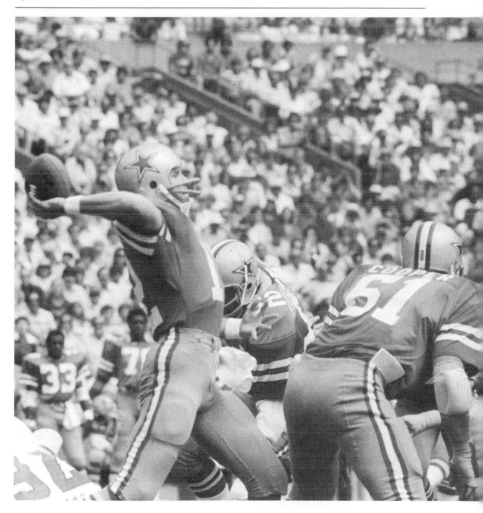

A badly separated shoulder suffered in an exhibition game limited Staubach to just four games in 1972. Morton took over once again and led the team to a 10-4 record. Near the end of the year, however, he came down with pneumonia. He started the divisional playoff game against the San Francisco 49ers, but with the Cowboys down 28-13, Landry replaced him with Staubach. Roger guided the team to a thrilling comeback as the Cowboys scored seventeen unanswered points in the fourth quarter to win 30-28. It was the type of comeback Staubach became known for over the course of his career. Unfortunately, Washington defeated Dallas in the NFC title game, and the team's bid for another Super Bowl fell short.

With another quarterback controversy brewing for 1973, Landry again named Staubach the starter. Roger justified his coach's decision by leading the league in passing, completing a career-high 62.6 percent of his attempts. He did so while suffering with the knowledge that his mother was dying of cancer. She passed away prior to the last regular season game, but Staubach still led his team to the NFC Championship game. Although they lost that game to Minnesota, his mental toughness and leadership won him even more respect from his teammates. As wide receiver Drew Pearson said, "Roger is the type of teammate, even though this tragedy happened in his life, he knew that his mother wanted him to continue to go out there and play. He didn't want his anguish, his grief, his problems to become our problems, and that's just the kind of guy he was."[63]

The "Hail Mary" Pass

The Cowboys failed to make the playoffs in 1974. A team-record twelve rookies—nicknamed the Dirty Dozen—made the club out of training camp in 1975. They injected the team with a dose of renewed enthusiasm. With Staubach at the helm the Cowboys surprised everyone by winning their first four games of the season. The Cowboys finished the year with a 10-4 record to give them the NFC wild card berth in the playoffs. In the division playoff, their opponent once again was Minnesota.

The Vikings had won the Central Division and were favored by eight points over Dallas. With less than a minute left to play in the game, Minnesota had a 14-10 lead. The Cowboys faced a fourth-

and-seventeen from their own 25-yard line. The situation looked bleak but the Cowboys did not give up. "With seconds to go," said linebacker Lee Roy Jordan, "we were a long way from scoring a touchdown, but I knew we still had a chance."[64]

On the next play Staubach rifled a pass that Drew Pearson caught for a first down at the 50-yard line. An incomplete pass followed, giving the Cowboys second-and-ten with thirty-six seconds left in the game. Dallas had no time-outs remaining, so the clock could not be stopped. The stage was set for the most famous play in Dallas Cowboys' history.

Staubach set up in the shotgun formation, an offensive formation in which the quarterback stands several yards behind the center in order to receive the snap. He faded back to pass, pump-faked once to decoy the defenders, then threw the ball deep to Pearson in the right corner of the field. The ball was slightly underthrown and Pearson had to slow down and turn in order to reach it. He described what happened next. "The ball hit right in my hands," he said. "Then [cornerback Nate Wright] hit my arm and the ball slipped but stuck between my elbow and hip. I just pulled it up and ran into the end zone."[65]

The Vikings claimed Pearson interfered with Wright, and both men admitted there was contact on the play. "We were both jousting, trying to get inside for the ball," admitted Pearson. "They could have called it on either one of us."[66] No flag was thrown, however, and the play stood. The Cowboys had pulled out a 17-14 victory, adding to Staubach's reputation. "Captain Comeback" had come to the rescue once again. In the process he also added a new term to football's lexicon. "After the game," said Roger, "reporters asked me about it and I said, 'I just closed my eyes and said a Hail Mary. . . .' Before, a play like that was described as an 'Alley-Oop.'"[67]

Near Misses

Following the victory over Minnesota, the Cowboys defeated the Los Angeles Rams in the NFC Championship game, but lost to the Pittsburgh Steelers in Super Bowl X. Staubach would collect another Super Bowl ring, however, before his NFL career ended. His fourth trip to football's biggest game was in Super Bowl XII against the Denver Broncos. He considered that year's Cowboys team the best one he played on in his eleven NFL seasons. Denver was led by former Dallas quarterback Craig Morton. The Broncos, however, were no match for the Cowboys, who defeated them by a score of 27-10. Staubach passed for 183 yards, completing seventeen of twenty-five passes with one touchdown and no interceptions.

The Cowboys made it back to the Super Bowl the following year, again matched up against the Pittsburgh Steelers. Each club was trying to become the first three-time Super Bowl winner. Staubach considered this the most disappointing game he ever played in. The two evenly matched teams battled back and forth for sixty minutes. Mistakes and bad breaks cost the Cowboys the game as Pittsburgh scored a 35-31 victory. Dallas had missed its chance to record back-to-back Super Bowl wins, while Pittsburgh gained recognition as the Team of the Seventies.

Throwing for 183 yards in his fourth Super Bowl, Roger Staubach led the Cowboys to victory over the Denver Broncos.

Injuries and retirements, particularly on defense, gave the Cowboys a new look for 1979. Coach Landry decided to open up the passing game, giving Staubach more opportunities to throw. The plan worked to perfection as the Cowboys won seven of their first eight games.

The ninth week, however, Dallas lost to the Steelers in a very physical game. At one point Pittsburgh's L. C. Greenwood tackled Staubach as he tried to scramble, and Roger hit his head hard on the ground. He was knocked unconscious and suffered a concussion. It was the most severe of the five concussions he had that year.

Despite the injuries Staubach did not miss a single game. He guided Dallas to an 11-5 season, recording career highs in completed passes (267), yards passing (3,586), and touchdown passes (27). The Cowboys won their fourth straight NFC East title but lost to the Los Angeles Rams 21-19 in the divisional playoff game.

However, the concussions finally took their toll. On March 31, 1980, at a press conference at Texas Stadium, Staubach surprised everyone by announcing his retirement after eleven years with the Cowboys. "I want to spend more time, more quality time, with my family," said Roger. "The concussions were somewhat of a factor, but not the overriding thing." [68]

Life after Football

In 1970, during Staubach's second season in Dallas, he had launched a career in real estate. He learned the business under commercial broker Henry S. Miller Jr. At the time, brokers were paid by the landlord while supposedly representing the tenant.

In 1978, Roger struck out to found his own real estate brokerage. He made an unprecedented decision to represent only tenants with his firm. He is currently chairman of the board and chief executive officer of The Staubach Company, a full-service real estate strategy and services firm that serves organizations seeking office, retail, and industrial space. It currently has thirty-six offices in thirty-one cities, and more than eight hundred employees.

Staubach's success as a businessman has allowed him to help others in many ways. One of those was former teammate Bob Hayes, who was battling a drug and alcohol addiction. Roger gave him a job and steered him toward an alcohol rehabilitation program. As Hayes recounted in his autobiography, "[Staubach] was determined to get me straight, and he saved my life." [69]

More Than Just a Great Player

Staubach left the NFL with an enviable record. He led the league in passing four times, was named to six Pro Bowls, and was named all-NFC four times. He will long be remembered as one of the most accurate passers of all time and as a courageous leader of men. His ability to pull out victories was legendary. His teammates had the utmost confidence in his ability to lead them to victory, even when defeat was staring them right in the face. Twenty-three times he led the Cowboys to come-from-behind wins in the last quarter, seventeen of those times in the final two minutes of the game. As teammate Billy Joe Dupree put it, "Roger never knew when the game was over." [70]

Hall of Famer Roger Staubach, far right, led the league in passing four times and was one of the most accurate passers in NFL history.

Staubach was elected to the Pro Football Hall of Fame in 1985, his first year of eligibility. Befitting the modest star, he said his biggest thrill came five years later when his coach was inducted. "Of all the wonderful experiences I had with the Cowboys," he said at the time, "being the presenter for Tom Landry at the Hall of Fame is the greatest thrill. That's because he asked me to represent all the players he coached. I'll be speaking for everyone, and that's a tremendous honor."[71]

Hayes's comments are perhaps the best tribute of all for one of the Cowboys' greatest players. "He is not only a teammate, a friend, and a neighbor," he said, "but one of the best men that I've ever met. . . . He cares for people, and I'm just lucky to have a man like him care about me."[72]

CHAPTER 6

Tony Dorsett

Tony Dorsett came out of the football hotbed of western Pennsylvania to become one of the game's all-time great running backs. A Heisman Trophy winner in college, he ranked second on the National Football League's list of career rushing leaders at the time of his retirement. Dorsett's contentious nature and confident swagger alienated many in the conservative Texas community. At the same time, his ball-carrying talents won him the admiration of millions in the football-crazed state. The love-hate relationship that developed between Dorsett and Cowboys fans is only part of the story of one of the more controversial players to wear a Dallas uniform.

From the Steel Mills to the Gridiron

Anthony Drew Dorsett was born in the steel-mill town of Aliquippa, Pennsylvania, just outside Pittsburgh, on April 7, 1954. The sixth of seven children born to Wes and Myrtle Dorsett, Anthony had four older brothers (Melvin, Ernie, Tyrone, and Keith), an older sister (Juanita), and a younger sister (Sheree). His parents were originally from North Carolina but settled in Pennsylvania during World War II. His father got a job working for Jones & Laughlin Steel and remained with the company for thirty years.

Tony's mother was the matriarch of the family, taking care of the house while her husband was at work.

The Dorsett family lived in the projects of Aliquippa in a neat, well-kept, two-story home. As the youngest son, Anthony was strictly watched over by his parents. They wanted to make sure he did not get into trouble, as his brothers often did. They encouraged him to do well in school in the hope he could avoid winding up

At the time of his retirement, Tony Dorsett was considered one of football's greatest running backs, ranking second on the all-time rushing list.

working in the dangerous mill. "The mill is not a place you want to go to," said his father. "At the mill, you go in, but you never know if you'll come out."[73]

Just as the mill was a way of life in Aliquippa, so too was football. It provided the means to a better future, a chance to go to college and perhaps follow in the path of Joe Namath, Mike Ditka, or one of the other pro stars who came from the region.

Quiet by nature, Anthony's sport of choice as a youngster was basketball. His brothers, however, encouraged him to play football as they did. They were his sports heroes. At first Tony was afraid of getting hurt, but his brothers, all of whom were very fast runners, teased him and egged him on. "Hey, man," said older brother Ernie, "you ain't gonna be anything. Your brothers have got speed, why don't you be like us?"[74]

As a sophomore at predominantly white Hopewell High School, Dorsett made the varsity football team. He was small for his age, but could run really fast. The first time he touched the ball in a game he returned a kickoff seventy-five yards for a touchdown.

While playing football, Anthony became more aggressive and developed a quick temper. One day he overheard two of his teachers talking about him. "That kid will turn out to be just like his brothers," said one. "The wildness is there now. . . . He's got lots of athletic talent like his brothers and he'll wind up just like them— nowhere."[75] Hearing this, Dorsett promised himself he would prove them wrong.

As a running back and defensive back, he led Hopewell to a 9-1 record in his junior year. In the team's only loss—to Sharon High School—Dorsett was hit in the head and forced to leave the game with what was diagnosed as a concussion. He was determined to get even for the hit. When the two teams met the next year, he rushed for a school record 247 yards and scored four touchdowns. His most satisfying game of all, however, was in the last game of his high school career. Playing against unbeaten Beaver Falls, Anthony rushed for 189 yards and scored three touchdowns. The 35-0 victory capped another 9-1 year for Hopewell.

By this time Dorsett was being recruited by more than a hundred colleges around the country. Anthony had originally planned on going to Penn State to play for coach Joe Paterno. He changed his mind, however, when he learned that Johnny Majors had been hired as head coach at the nearby University of Pittsburgh. The football team at the University of Pittsburgh had been in decline for some years. Coach Majors made it known that he intended to turn the program around and do his best to make the school a national powerhouse. He let Dorsett know that he was the kind of player he could build his program around. Anthony believed Majors. On February 17, 1973, he signed a letter of intent to attend the University of Pittsburgh.

Dorsett signed his letter of intent to attend the University of Pittsburgh after learning Johnny Majors had been named head coach.

A Record-Setting College Career

On his first play in his first scrimmage, Dorsett took a handoff and ran eighty yards for a touchdown. By the third day of practice he won the position of starting tailback. Hopes for the football team began to grow.

Around this time Anthony was approached by Dean Billik, the school's sports information director, with a rather unusual request. "We think it's a good idea to call you Tony Dorsett," said Billik. "Tony 'T.D.' Dorsett, for 'touchdowns.' It will give you and Pitt [the university] more of an identity."[76] At first Dorsett didn't like the name change, having always preferred Anthony. He went along with it, however, in order to help the school.

Prior to his first game as a Panther, Tony faced a personal crisis. His girlfriend became pregnant and he contemplated leaving school. His mother urged him to put an end to such thoughts. "You're supposed to be a grown man now," she said. "You only get this one chance once in a lifetime."[77] After discussing the matter further with assistant coach Jackie Sherrill, Dorsett decided to stay.

Dorsett's first game at Pitt was on September 15, 1973, the day his girlfriend gave birth to Anthony Jr. That day Tony ran for 103 yards as the Panthers held nationally ranked Georgia to a 10-10 tie.

It was only the beginning. Against Northwestern, Dorsett rushed for an incredible 365 yards. Several weeks later he ran for 209 against Notre Dame. This was especially impressive since Notre Dame's defense had allowed an average of just 59 yards rushing per game in the seven weeks prior to the meeting. Notre Dame head coach Ara Parseghian was moved to say, "Dorsett's a remarkable football player. I didn't think anybody could make that kind of yardage against us."[78]

Tony had many other similar games in his career at Pitt. As a 155-pound freshman he ran for 1,686 yards, shattering the all-time first-year rushing record. He was named to the all-American team for the first of four times. By his senior season he was a solid 192 pounds. He became the first college player to surpass the thousand-yard mark in each of his four years of eligibility. He ran for 1,948 yards his senior year, giving him a record total of 6,082 for his career. In his final game at Pitt he rushed for 202 yards to lead the Panthers to a 27-3 win over Georgia in the Sugar Bowl.

After rushing for 6,082 collegiate career yards and 202 in his final game against Georgia in the Sugar Bowl, Dorsett won the Heisman Trophy.

The victory gave Pitt the national championship with a perfect 12-0 record. For his performance that season Tony won the Heisman Trophy as the outstanding college football player in the nation.

Next Stop, Dallas

On draft day in 1977, the Dallas Cowboys traded four draft picks to the Seattle Seahawks to get the second pick in the draft. With that pick they selected Tony Dorsett. Opposing general managers shook their heads in disbelief. Said Ernie Accorsi of the Baltimore

Colts, "The Cowboys got themselves a Hall of Famer for four draft choices."[79]

In his four years at Pitt, Dorsett's outgoing, fun-loving personality began to emerge. He enjoyed having a good time and developed a flair that was unmistakable. Having signed a three-year, $1.6 million contract with the Cowboys, he now was able to express himself in a manner previously impossible. He bought his parents a new house and spent some money on himself. When he showed up at Dallas's training camp he was driving a black Porsche and wearing a full-length mink coat.

His flashy appearance and behavior did not sit well with some members of the Dallas community. In his first week with the team he was involved in a racially motivated incident in a local disco bar. Dorsett was arrested on two counts of simple assault but all charges were eventually dropped. The negative publicity, however, helped build an image that was hard to overcome. Trouble seemed to follow him, much of it not of his own making. As teammate Roger Staubach recounted, "It's true Tony caused some of his own problems. But being an outspoken black man in Dallas wasn't easy then. It made things worse. . . . If he had been white, perhaps a lot of what happened would have been overlooked."[80]

On the playing field things were not going the way Tony had envisioned. He did not play much during the first few games of the regular season, as coach Tom Landry wanted to gradually move him into a starting role. Landry wanted Tony to be more intense in practice and show his desire to win a starting job. However, Dorsett was easing off, figuring he would have to wait until the next year for his chance. The miscommunication between the two caused a bit of friction, but things were eventually worked out. Dorsett made his first start of the year against the Pittsburgh Steelers in the tenth game of the season. Less than a month later, on December 4, 1977, Tony rushed for a team-record 206 yards against the Philadelphia Eagles. Included was a touchdown run of eighty-four yards, the longest Dallas run from scrimmage ever.

The game sparked Dorsett to a strong finish. He ended the year as the first Cowboy rookie to rush for over a thousand yards (1,007) and set a Dallas record for most rushing touchdowns in a season with twelve. "Tony Dorsett made a *big* difference when he came in '77," recalled Staubach. "This guy was a sensational player. He had speed, and he was tough, could run inside. He took a lot of the pressure off me."[81] Dorsett's value to the team was underscored when he was named NFL Offensive Rookie of the Year.

With Dorsett having played a key role, Dallas won the NFC East title and began postseason play. Tony scored four touchdowns in three Cowboys' victories as the team made its run to Super Bowl XII. There, before more than seventy-five thousand fans in the Louisiana Superdome, Tony scored the first touchdown of the game and went on to gain sixty-six yards rushing in the Cowboys' 27-10 win over the Denver Broncos. Dorsett had won a Super Bowl ring in his very first professional season, the perfect way to end his rookie year as a Cowboy.

The Emergence of a Star

Dorsett's second season with Dallas proved eventful. During the year two threats were made against his life by people in the conservative Dallas area who resented the success of a young, outspoken African-American. Dorsett never hesitated to speak his mind when it came to things with which he disagreed. He rebelled against what he considered the inflexible discipline of coach Landry. The day before the Philadelphia Eagles' game in October, Dorsett overslept and missed a practice. Landry told him he would not start the game and might not play at all. Dorsett was furious since his parents had made the trip to Dallas to see him play. He did get to play late in the game but never forgot the incident.

Despite these distractions, Dorsett continued to produce on the playing field. He gained 1,325 yards rushing for the season and led Dallas to another appearance in the Super Bowl. This time, however, the Cowboys came out on the losing end, falling to the Pittsburgh Steelers 35-31.

Over the following seasons Dorsett broke one record after another. After gaining 1,107 yards on the ground in 1979, he piled up 1,185 the next year. By doing so he became the first running back in NFL history to rush for more than a thousand yards in each of his first four seasons. That same year he set a team playoff record on December 26 with 160 yards rushing against the Los Angeles Rams.

In 1981, in only his fifth season in the league, he passed Don Perkins to become Dallas's all-time leading rusher. He gained a career-high 1,646 yards on the year, and had nine games of one hundred or more yards rushing. The next year he led the NFC in rushing, gaining 745 yards in the strike-shortened nine-game season.

A Record-Setting Run

Dorsett's most memorable moment of all occurred on January 3, 1983. The Cowboys were playing the Minnesota Vikings that night in the final regular season game at the Metrodome in Minneapolis. A *Monday Night Football* audience watched the Vikings score late in the fourth quarter to take a 24-13 lead. On the ensuing kickoff, Dallas's Timmy Newsome fumbled and the ball went out of bounds at the Cowboys' 1-yard line.

Dorsett was on the sidelines when he heard the next play called, a play he knew was designed for him. He raced onto the field, yelling at fullback Ron Springs, "Ron, Ron, Ron! Get to the bench! Get out! Get out!"[82] Springs ran to the sidelines, leaving the

On December 26, 1979, Tony Dorsett set a team playoff record for rushing with 160 yards against the Los Angeles Rams.

Cowboys with just ten men on the field instead of eleven. When he realized what had happened, Springs stayed there rather than risk a penalty by not getting back in time.

The Vikings were bunched together in a short-yardage defense (most of the defensive players positioned near the line, assuming the play to be a run rather than a pass). Dorsett took the handoff from quarterback Danny White and, following a block, burst up the middle. He cut toward the sideline and sprinted into the open field. Two Minnesota defenders and teammate Drew Pearson were the only ones standing between him and the end zone. With a burst of speed Dorsett broke past them as Pearson took out one Viking with a block. The other defender pushed Tony, but Dorsett managed to keep his balance and continue on for a touchdown. The play covered ninety-nine yards, making it the longest run from scrimmage in NFL history. It is a record that may someday be tied but can never be broken.

Despite the moments of personal glory that Dorsett experienced, the Cowboys could not make it back to the Super Bowl in any of those seasons. While still one of the league's better teams, Dallas was beginning to show signs of aging.

Hard Times

The mid-1980s were a time of personal upheaval for Dorsett. In 1983 his name was brought up in connection with a federal drug investigation. Since he was known to enjoy the nightlife and was highly visible, he was an easy target. The investigation was eventually abandoned and no charges were ever brought against him. The damage had already been done, however, and the stigma remained.

The next year Dorsett's three-year marriage to Julie Simon began to fall apart. He realized that he hadn't married for love but rather for companionship. Their divorce became final in 1985. In the midst of his marital problems Tony received word that his father had suffered a stroke and fallen into a coma. Wes Dorsett died shortly afterward.

Tony's troubles continued in the summer of 1985. First, he lost money in an oil exploration deal pushed by his agent. That was followed by a bill for over four hundred thousand dollars in back taxes from the Internal Revenue Service. During the same period

Dorsett was involved in renegotiating his contract with the Cowboys. After a twenty-one-day holdout the team finally gave in. Dorsett received a twenty-year annuity worth $6 million, similar to the deal received by star defensive tackle Randy White.

Throughout these troublesome times Dorsett continued to produce on the field. He passed the thousand-yard mark for rushing in each of those seasons, recording 1,321 in 1983, 1,189 in 1984, and 1,307 in 1985. On October 13, 1985, he became just the sixth running back in NFL history to reach the ten-thousand-yard plateau.

In August of the next year, however, the Cowboys made a move that did not bode well for Dorsett's future with the team. They signed Heisman Trophy winner Herschel Walker to a $5 million, five-year contract. Although fans fantasized about the "dream backfield" of Walker and Dorsett, it seemed obvious to many that the younger Walker was the future for Dallas.

The End of the Line

In 1987 the NFL players went on strike again in an attempt to gain free agency (the chance to choose which team to play for when their contract ran out). When Randy White crossed the picket line, Dorsett spoke out, calling him "Captain Scab." Later, however, after being informed by the team that he would lose his annuity if he stayed out, Tony felt he had no choice but to return. As he said, "That period was the weirdest in my life. I was one of the union spearheads, then I walked through the line—with egg on my face. I hated it."[83]

When the strike finally ended and things returned to normal, Dorsett found his playing time reduced, in part, he believed, because of his involvement in the strike. On November 15 he did not start the game at tailback for the first time since his rookie season eleven years before. Later that year he did not play at all in a game against the Miami Dolphins.

Dorsett was angry and frustrated. He went to the Dallas front office and demanded a trade. The following June he got his wish and was sent to the Denver Broncos in exchange for a draft pick. In explaining the deal, Broncos coach Dan Reeves said of Dorsett, "He is one of those players who, no matter where he goes, brings his team up to a new level. Above everything else, Tony Dorsett is a winner."[84]

Unfortunately, Tony was unable to turn back the clock with Denver. As age began to catch up with him, he rushed for just 703 yards in 1988 while the Broncos struggled to an 8-8 record. The next year he suffered torn knee ligaments during training camp and was forced to retire. He ended his career as the second-leading rusher in NFL history.

Life After Football

Since retiring from football Dorsett has tried his hand at several different businesses in the Dallas area. He runs a successful specialty marketing firm, does promotional work for Sprint, does a weekly football preview show for Player's Box, and is a cochairman of the Texas Black Hall of Fame.

Much of Dorsett's time since his retirement has been spent following the career of his son, Anthony Jr. Of course, like any proud parent, he's always more than willing to offer any advice to help his son. Anthony is a defensive back who was drafted by the Houston Oilers in 1996. Following the 1999 season he started in Super Bowl XXXIV. In doing so the Dorsetts became only the third father-son combination to reach the Super Bowl, and the only one where each started the game.

Despite the many hardships he has endured over the years—including the deaths of a brother, his father, and a fiancée—Tony has found peace and happiness. "If life got any better," he said during an interview, "they would have to make me a twin. . . . I'm very happy in all aspects. My business is good. My home life is wonderful. I'm just a happy man." [85]

An Impressive Legacy

Adding to Dorsett's happiness were several prestigious honors that came his way. He was elected to both the college and pro football halls of fame in 1994. In December 1999 he was named to the Walter Camp all-century college football team. Some of the rushing records he set have been broken, including his college career mark by Ricky Williams and the Cowboys career mark by Emmitt Smith. Tony, however, has no regrets. "People keep asking me, how do I feel about the records," says Dorsett. "I don't feel anything. You realize that records are made to be broken. It's nice to have a record. That says something about the career itself. But what I appreciate is the guys doing their thing. Ricky and Emmitt

Inducted into the Hall of Fame, Dorsett will be remembered for his speed, power, and ability to hit holes and outrun pursuers.

are quality guys. You can't help but wish for the best for them. If that means breaking records of Tony Dorsett, so be it."[86]

Those who saw him play will remember Dorsett's speed and power, his ability to hit holes in the line and outrun his pursuers. An important cog in the Cowboys' teams of the 1980s, he was a perfect complement to the Dallas passing game. As such, his place in football history has been assured.

CHAPTER 7

Troy Aikman

When the Green Bay Packers rallied to defeat the Phoenix Cardinals 26-17 on the last weekend of the 1988 season, few Dallas Cowboys fans could have imagined the dramatic effect it would have on the future of their team. By doing so, the Packers posted their fourth win of the season. The Cowboys, with just three victories, were thus assured of the first overall pick in the following spring's NFL draft. With that selection they chose UCLA's all-American quarterback Troy Aikman. Despite a series of injuries that shortened his career, Aikman's leadership and talents, particularly his strong, accurate arm, eventually led the Cowboys out of the doldrums and back to the top of the NFL standings, in the process adding another chapter to the story of America's Team.

From California to Oklahoma

Troy Kenneth Aikman was born in the sunny climate of West Covina, California, on November 21, 1966. The future All-Pro quarterback did not have an easy childhood. He was born with a deformity of both feet, one his mother described as "one-third club feet."[87] His legs were encased in casts up to his knees from the time he was eight months old until he started to walk six months later. After that he had to wear orthopedic shoes until he was three. In order to help keep his feet straight, Troy's mother had to strap the heels of his shoes together at night while he slept.

Eventually the problem was corrected, and together with his father Kenneth, his mother Charlyn, and his two older sisters, Tammy and Terri, Troy enjoyed an active life in southern California. He was a star pitcher on his Little League baseball team and dreamed of someday pitching for the Los Angeles Dodgers.

With his strong, accurate arm, Troy Aikman led the Cowboys out of the doldrums and back to dominance.

When he was twelve years old, however, his father got a job working on an oil pipeline. The family moved to a 172-acre ranch in Henryetta, Oklahoma, where they raised chickens, pigs, and cattle. The decision to move hit Troy hard. "To be quite honest with you," he recalled, "I was not looking forward to it."[88] He made the adjustment well, however, and within a few short months came to appreciate life in the town of sixty-five hundred people.

In order to fit in with his new friends, Troy decided to try out for his junior high school football team. He began his football career as a fullback but was soon switched to quarterback when his outstanding arm strength became apparent. He led his ninth-grade team to a 7-1 record.

At Henryetta High School, Troy's strong arm helped him win the starting quarterback position as a fourteen-year-old sophomore. Unfortunately, he was not surrounded by above-average talent. The Fighting Hens finished with a 4-6 record that year, then followed up with marks of 2-9 and 6-4 the next two seasons.

Aikman also played baseball at Henryetta, excelling as a catcher and shortstop. The New York Mets showed interest in drafting him, but were turned off when he said he would not sign for less than two hundred thousand dollars. They did not know that he had promised his father he would attend college, and had given them a high price with the intention of discouraging them.

Difficult Decisions

With professional baseball now out of the picture, Aikman turned his attention to deciding which college he would attend. He was recruited by many top football programs, including Oklahoma State and the University of Oklahoma. (As luck would have it, the head coaches at the two schools were Jimmy Johnson and Barry Switzer respectively, both of whom would later coach him with the Cowboys.) Troy finally decided on Oklahoma when Switzer said he would change the team's wishbone offense to take better advantage of Aikman's strong arm and unerring accuracy as a passer. (The wishbone, a formation in which the halfbacks line up farther from the line of scrimmage than the fullback is better suited for a quarterback who has running as opposed to passing skills.)

After a lackluster freshman year Aikman began his sophomore season by leading the Sooners to victories in their first three games. Against Miami, however, he suffered a broken ankle, putting an

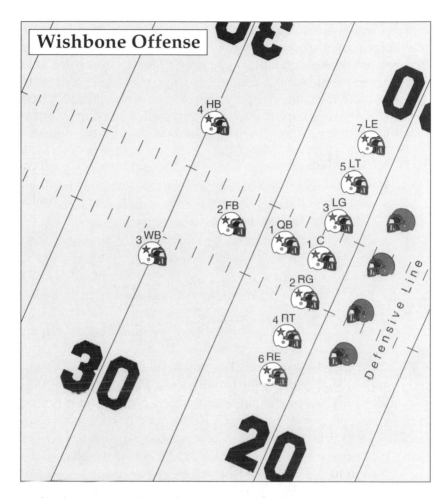

end to his season. His replacement was freshman Jamelle Holieway. Switzer returned to the wishbone and the fleet-footed Holieway led the team to the national championship. The next season Aikman was Holieway's backup, even though Switzer admitted that Aikman would be a better NFL player. Holieway, however, was a better fit for Oklahoma's wishbone offense.

Realizing he would need more exposure in order to attract NFL scouts, Aikman decided to transfer. Switzer helped him get into UCLA, where coach Terry Donahue was only too happy to have the six-foot four-inch junior. "The first time I saw him throw," recalled the coach, "I knew he had a great arm and that we had a great player."[89]

After sitting out a year because of transfer eligibility rules, Aikman led UCLA to consecutive 10-2 seasons in 1987 and 1988. He finished each year with a bowl game win. During his senior year Aikman won the Davey O'Brien Award, given annually to the top quarterback in the country. Many people were now calling him the best quarterback prospect since Stanford's all-American John Elway in 1983. His prospects in the pro ranks looked bright indeed.

On to Dallas

By virtue of having the worst record in the National Football League in 1988, the Cowboys had the first overall pick in the 1989 college draft. They surprised no one when they selected Aikman, who they hoped would be the key to the team's resurgence. They quickly signed him to a six-year contract worth $11 million, the most money ever for a first-year player. Troy appreciated his good fortune. Before he even played a game for Dallas, he established yearly five-thousand-dollar scholarships at both Henryetta High School and UCLA. In addition, he said he would donate one thousand dollars to charity for every Dallas victory.

Before he could start earning his money, however, he had to win a starting job. That summer the Cowboys used a special first-round pick in the NFL supplemental draft to select another high-profile quarterback, Steve Walsh of the University of Miami. Rather than complain about this unexpected competition, Troy simply went about his business and worked extra hard to show the coaches he could lead the team. When it came time for the opening game of the regular season, Aikman was the starting quarterback.

Unfortunately, Cowboy victories were hard to come by in 1989. Rookies had replaced many of the older players and their inexperience showed. The Cowboys won just one game in sixteen played. Troy missed their one victory when he was out for a month with a broken finger. The highlight of his season came the week he returned to action. Playing against the Phoenix Cardinals, Aikman threw for 379 yards, setting an NFL single-game rookie record. After throwing the go-ahead touchdown with less than two minutes remaining, however, he was knocked unconscious and had to be helped from the field. The Cardinals came back to score and sent the Cowboys to another defeat.

Although not spectacular, Aikman's numbers for his first NFL season were not at all bad. He made the roster on most of the media's all-rookie teams and showed promise of becoming an excellent quarterback, earning the respect of his teammates as a leader on the field. Physically, however, he had taken a beating. Said Aikman, "I was so badly beaten up that I couldn't understand how some of my teammates had lasted ten years in the NFL. I knew I'd never make it that long. There was nothing fun about football. It was time for a gut check."[90]

A Team on the Rise

In the meantime, coach Jimmy Johnson was doing his best to surround Aikman with better players by making trades and acquiring draft choices. The results began to show in 1990. The offense was much improved, with NFL Rookie of the Year Emmitt Smith contributing to the mix. Aikman posted his first NFL victory in an early season, come-from-behind win over the San Diego Chargers. He led the team to seven victories before suffering a separated shoulder in the next-to-last game of the season. With Aikman on the sidelines, Dallas lost its final two games to finish at 7-9.

Dallas's offense was built around Aikman, running back Smith, and wide receiver Michael Irvin. It was obvious that the Cowboys would score points. Equally obvious to Johnson was the fact that he had to provide better protection for his quarterback. Through draft picks, trades, and free agency he was able to put together a formidable offensive line for 1991. The Cowboys also began to use a "quick-release" passing offense, which meant that defenders would have less time to get to Aikman. As offensive coordinator Norv Turner explained, "I shortened the [wide receivers'] routes, cut down the steps on his drops, and based everything on quick timing."[91]

The tactics proved successful. Troy threw for 2,754 yards, completed 65 percent of his passes, and saw his interceptions total drop from eighteen to ten. The numbers translated into eleven wins for the Cowboys, and a spot in the postseason playoffs for the first time in six years. Unfortunately, injury again cut Aikman's playing time short. A sprained knee caused him to miss four regular season games and one playoff contest.

The potential Aikman had shown in his first three years was ready to blossom. Former Dallas Hall of Fame quarterback Roger

With a "quick-release" passing offense built around Troy Aikman (8), Michael Irvin (88), and Emmitt Smith (22), the Cowboys became a powerhouse.

Staubach saw a Super Bowl in the Cowboys' near future with Aikman at the controls. Staubach proved to be as accurate with his predictions as he had been with his passes.

A Dream Season

In 1992, Troy Aikman established himself as one of the National Football League's top quarterbacks. He guided the Cowboys to a 13-3 record in the regular season, finishing third in NFL passer ratings, and threw for career highs in total passing yardage (3,445) and touchdown passes (23). In one game against the Atlanta Falcons, he completed 18 of 21 passes, including 13 in a row, for an incredible 85.7 completion percentage.

As good as he was in the regular season, Aikman was even better in the playoffs. In victories over the Philadelphia Eagles and San Francisco 49ers he completed 39 of 59 passes (66.1 percent) for 522 yards, four touchdowns, and no interceptions.

Aikman continued his magic in Super Bowl XXVII against the Buffalo Bills. He methodically picked apart the Buffalo defense, completing 22 of 30 passes for 273 yards and four touchdowns, again with no interceptions. As running back Emmitt Smith explained, "Troy was definitely in a zone. Once he had time, he picked out his receivers accordingly and got the ball to them and let them be runners after that."[92]

Dallas took advantage of a Super Bowl–record nine Buffalo turnovers to rout the Bills by a score of 52-17 for its first Super Bowl victory since 1977. For his part, Aikman was named the game's most valuable player. In four short seasons he had led the Cowboys from the bottom of the NFL standings to the top. He had every intention of helping them stay in that position.

Remaining Champs

Many players believe that remaining champions is even harder than reaching that exalted level for the first time. In 1993, Aikman and the Cowboys showed everyone that it was indeed possible. The year began with Dallas owner Jerry Jones reaffirming his confidence in his quarterback by signing him to a new eight-year deal that would pay him $50 million. It made Troy the highest-paid player in NFL history.

By his performance, Aikman showed that he was worth every penny. The Cowboys won the NFC East title for the second consecutive season, compiling a 12-4 record. Troy's 69.1 percent completion average was the fourth-best mark in league history, while his 99.0 passer rating was his career high. The year was not without its bad moments, however. An injury once again caused him to miss a pair of games.

In the postseason Aikman threw for 302 yards to lead the Cowboys to victory over the Green Bay Packers. In the NFC Championship game against the San Francisco 49ers he helped Dallas build a 28-7 lead. In the third quarter, however, he suffered a concussion and had to be removed from the game. With his status for the Super Bowl in doubt, he returned to the practice field five days later despite suffering from headaches and dizziness. He recovered in time to guide the team to a 30-13 win over the Buffalo Bills for its second consecutive Super Bowl victory. In doing so, Aikman became, at age twenty-seven, the youngest quarterback in league history to win a pair of championships.

Back on Top

The transfer of power from coach Jimmy Johnson to Barry Switzer in 1994 did not affect Aikman's on-field performance. Another sprained knee, however, did cause him to miss two games. Despite that, he still led Dallas to another 12-4 record and another NFC East championship. In the National Football Conference divisional playoff game against the Green Bay Packers, Aikman connected with Alvin Harper on a ninety-four-yard touchdown pass to set an NFL postseason record. The Cowboys romped past Green Bay, 35-9, then traveled to San Francisco for the conference championship game against the 49ers.

Aikman and coach Jimmy Johnson embrace after winning their second consecutive Super Bowl against the Buffalo Bills.

Another Super Bowl was not to be, however. Aikman threw for 380 yards against the 49ers, but was intercepted three times. When the smoke cleared, the Cowboys were on the short end of a 38-21 score. Their quest for another Super Bowl would have to wait another year.

In many ways the 1995 season was one of Aikman's most satisfying. He completed nearly 65 percent of his pass attempts and logged the second-highest passing rating of his career while leading the team to its third 12-4 record—and fourth NFC East title—in a row. He played in all sixteen games for only the second time in his career, although he was forced out of two games by injuries.

In the postseason Aikman led the Cowboys to an NFL-record eighth conference championship by defeating the Green Bay Packers. Dallas moved on to its eighth Super Bowl, three more than any other team. Troy led the team to a 27-17 victory over the Pittsburgh Steelers, consistently hitting his receivers with his passes. "Every time he throws the ball," said tight end Jay Novacek admiringly, "it's always a perfect throw. That's hard to get from any other quarterback."[93]

The win gave Dallas its third Super Bowl title in four seasons, something even the Pittsburgh Steelers and San Francisco 49ers powerhouse teams were unable to accomplish. In winning eleven of the thirteen postseason games he appeared in, Aikman had earned a reputation as a "big game" quarterback. His teammates had no doubt that he would continue to be successful. "With Troy," said Emmitt Smith, "we've always got the foundation. It all starts with the quarterback, and we've got a great one. We have confidence in him. I don't see why we can't keep winning as long as we stay healthy."[94] Unfortunately, staying healthy is sometimes beyond a player's control.

The Post–Super Bowl Years

In the years following Super Bowl XXX, Dallas fell on difficult times. Only twice in the next five years did the Cowboys win more than they lost. Overall, their regular season record was 39-41. In that time they won only one of four playoff contests.

Up until 2000, Aikman continued to put up solid numbers, even with his team on the decline. He holds, or is tied for, forty-five Dallas passing marks including club records for attempts (4,453), completions (2,742), passing yards (31,310), touchdowns (158), and completion percentage (61.6). In recognition of his contributions to the Cowboys' success, he was rewarded in 1998 with a new $85.5 million contract, again making him the highest-paid player in the National Football League. Ironically, the contract was one of the factors that led to his eventual departure from Dallas.

Over the course of twelve seasons, Aikman paid a great toll physically. He suffered from back problems that occasionally required him to receive injections of painkillers. In 2000 he missed five games because of injuries and was knocked out of three more in the first quarter. On December 10 his season ended after a bone-crushing tackle by Washington Redskins linebacker LaVar Arrington. Aikman suffered his eleventh concussion—the ninth since entering the NFL, second of the season, and fourth in his last nineteen starts.

The effect of these injuries could be seen in Troy's reduced effectiveness. He was the lowest-rated quarterback in the National Football Conference in 2000. In a start against the New York Giants on October 15 he threw for a career-worst five interceptions.

During the off-season, Cowboys owner Jerry Jones faced a difficult dilemma: Could the Cowboys afford to begin the 2001 season with an expensive, fragile, thirty-four-year-old quarterback? After much soul-searching, he decided the answer was no. On March 7, 2001, he called a press conference to announce that Troy Aikman had been placed on waivers for the purpose of giving him his release. "This organization will forever be indebted for his contributions, his class, his leadership and his very deep appreciation for this organization and this community," said the Dallas owner. "Although he'll be missed on the field at Texas Stadium, he'll always be a Dallas Cowboy." [95]

Aikman wanted to continue playing for Dallas, but money presented a problem. If he remained on the roster past March 7, his contract called for him to receive a $7 million bonus and an extension through the year 2007. In addition, due to the rules dealing with the NFL's salary cap (which limits the amount of money a team can spend in a season), the team would have had a problem signing other players in the future.

Aikman understood the problems his remaining with the team would have presented. "It wasn't in the best interest of the ballclub to try doing that," he admitted.[96] However, he still felt he could be a productive player. "I'm still capable of going out and playing at a high level," he insisted, "and being healthy and doing the things necessary to be productive."[97] Aikman hoped to sign with another team, possibly the San Diego Chargers, where former Cowboys' offensive coordinator Norv Turner was on the staff. Unfortunately, such was not to be. On April 9, 2001, he announced his retirement.

With his good looks and knowledge of the game, Troy is a natural for television. Some years ago he did color commentary on NFL Europe broadcasts. He will likely be spending a great deal more time in front of the camera in the future.

Aikman is helped off the field after suffering his ninth concussion in the NFL. The injury eventually led to his retirement.

A Future Hall of Famer

As great as his contributions on the field have been, Aikman will also be remembered for his activities outside of football. In 1992 he founded the Troy Aikman Foundation to provide financial support for disadvantaged children in the Dallas–Fort Worth area. The foundation is currently concerned with creating Aikman End Zones in children's hospitals in the area. The End Zones are interactive playrooms and theaters designed to ease the hospital stay of critically ill children.

Troy has also authored a children's book—*Things Change*—the profits from which go to the foundation. He has given his time and effort to many other charitable causes and was the recipient of the Byron "Whizzer" White Humanitarian Award in 1994. The award is the NFL Players Association's most prestigious honor, given to the one player each year who best exemplifies the ideals personified by the former Supreme Court justice.

Aikman left behind a record as one of the top quarterbacks of all time. With a total of ninety regular season wins, he finished the 1990s with the most victories of any quarterback in any decade in the history of the league. (Joe Montana of the San Francisco 49ers is next with eighty-six wins in the 1980s.) Aikman is also one of only three men to lead his team to three Super Bowl victories. (Terry Bradshaw of the Pittsburgh Steelers and Montana are the others.)

Cowboy fans will remember Troy Aikman for a long, long time. Many will show up in Canton, Ohio, at some future date when he follows Roger Staubach to become the second Dallas quarterback inducted into the Pro Football Hall of Fame.

CHAPTER 8

Emmitt Smith

By National Football League standards, Emmitt Smith is small for a running back. However, at five-feet nine-inches tall and 205 pounds, he has risen to the top as one of the greatest running backs in the history of the game. Height and weight can both be measured; the will to succeed, however, cannot. Smith's talent, determination, and strength of character give him the ability to dominate a game, an ability that has helped lift the Dallas Cowboys from the bottom of the league standings to three Super Bowl championships.

A Star in the Making

Emmitt Smith was born on May 15, 1969, in Pensacola, Florida, to Emmitt Jr. and Mary Smith. His father was a city bus driver while his mother stayed home to care for Emmitt, his older sister Marsha, and his three younger brothers, Erik, Emory, and Emil. His parents were not well-off financially and the family lived in a government housing project. However, they provided their children with things that were more important than money. Emmitt later recalled, "I learned how to love, how to behave, how to give respect and earn it. Nothing in life, including pro football, means as much to me as they do."[98]

Emmitt Smith's talent, determination, and strength of character give him the ability to dominate a football game.

His mother also had a sharp eye. When Emmitt was just an infant, she turned on a football game and placed him in front of the television. As he relates in his autobiography, "Even at such a young age, my mom says, my eyes would follow the motion. Then I'd watch even closer when something exciting happened."[99]

Emmitt's father had been a football star in high school. Bad knees kept him from advancing any further, however, and he went to work driving a bus right after high school. He introduced his son to organized football at an early age. Emmitt played his first game at the age of eight. Because of his running ability he usually played against older kids. His experience in Pensacola's youth leagues prepared him for Escambia High School, where he starred as a running back for coach Dwight Thomas.

Right from the beginning, Emmitt gave evidence of being something special. His excellent peripheral vision and rapid acceleration enabled him to find holes in the line and burst through them before opponents could grab him. He gained 115 yards and scored two touchdowns in his very first game as a freshman. He helped carry the team to a 7-3 mark that season, a significant improvement from their 1-9 record of the previous year. Emmitt also played basketball, but soon gave the sport up in order to concentrate on football. By his sophomore year, he was already attracting the attention of local colleges.

In Emmitt's four years at Escambia the Gators won two state championships. Although the team failed to do so in Emmitt's senior season, he was named *Parade* magazine's high school player of the year. He ran for a total of 8,804 yards in his four years, scored 106 touchdowns, and averaged nearly eight yards per carry. Surprisingly, because he wasn't a power back or breakaway runner, some still questioned his ability. One well-known recruiting "expert" wrote, "Emmitt isn't a franchise player. He's a lugger, not a runner. Sportswriters blew him all out of proportion."[100] This person did not take into account his consistency, durability, and will to win.

Preparing for the Professional Ranks

Most colleges, however, disagreed with that "expert's" analysis. By the time he was a senior, Smith had been recruited by many of the nation's top schools. He narrowed his choices down to Auburn, Nebraska, and Florida. His family made sure he kept his priorities in order. "Go wherever you want to," advised his father. "Just make sure you study."[101] Emmitt eventually decided upon Florida based on a combination of factors including its football program, its location in nearby Gainesville, and its academic reputation.

It didn't take Smith long to make a splash with the Gators. He made his first start in the third game of his freshman year in a nationally televised contest against Alabama. Emmitt carried the ball thirty-nine times, gained 224 yards for a new Florida single-game record, and scored two touchdowns as the Gators upset the Crimson Tide. Emmitt passed the thousand-yard mark in rushing in Florida's seventh game of the year, faster than any runner in college football history.

Coach Galen Hall's squad finished the year with a 6-5 record, then lost to UCLA in the postseason Aloha Bowl. Smith's 1,341 yards rushing helped him to a ninth-place finish in the voting for the Heisman Trophy.

A knee injury in the sixth game of the season interrupted Smith's sophomore year. However, Florida again finished 6-5, defeating Illinois in the All-American Bowl. The next year, coach Hall resigned in midseason amid rumors of recruiting violations. The team eventually finished at 7-4, with Emmitt gaining 1,599 yards. After the season, offensive coordinator Whitey Jordan also left. With two men who had played a large part in his success now out of the picture, Smith decided to leave school early. College juniors were eligible for the National Football League's annual draft for the first time that April. Smith decided to try his luck as a professional.

The Cowboys' Hope

Ever since he was a boy in Pensacola, Emmitt's favorite professional football team had been the Dallas Cowboys. In April 1990 his dream came true: Dallas selected him with the seventeenth pick in the first round of the NFL draft. At the press conference introducing him to the media, Cowboys owner Jerry Jones explained how getting Emmitt would improve the team. "This is a bright spot," he said. "It's going to make [guard] Nate Newton block better, make [quarterback] Troy [Aikman] throw better, and make that defense a lot better, having this guy on our squad." [102] "Emmitt Smith brings star quality to us," added coach Jimmy Johnson. [103] It was obvious that the team needed all the help it could get: It had finished the previous season with a record of 1-15.

Smith missed most of training camp while contract negotiations between his agent and the Cowboys stalled. He finally signed five days before the season opener against the San Diego Chargers. Emmitt did not see much action in the first four games of the season. With the Cowboys' record at 1-3, however, he was given his first start against the Tampa Bay Buccaneers. He carried the ball twenty-three times, gaining 121 yards and helping Dallas to a 14-10 victory.

In the second half of the season the Cowboys began to come together, at one point winning four games in a row. They narrowly missed making the playoffs and finished with a record of 7-9. Smith compiled impressive numbers his rookie season, gaining 937 yards on the ground and scoring eleven touchdowns, including four in a game against the Phoenix Cardinals. For his efforts Smith was named the NFL Offensive Rookie of the Year by the Associated Press.

The next season Norv Turner replaced David Shula as the Cowboys' offensive coordinator. He promised Smith that he would be even more involved in Dallas's offense, getting more carries than he had the previous year. Turner was true to his word. In the Cowboys' very first game of the season, Smith carried the ball a career-high thirty-two times and caught six passes. The thirty-eight times he handled the ball was a record for a Dallas running back. Emmitt continued his heavy workload, and after four weeks of play he was at the top of the league's rushing charts for the very first time.

Dallas finished the 1991 season with five consecutive victories and found itself in the playoffs for the first time in six years. Smith led the National Football League in rushing with 1,563 yards, becoming—at age twenty-two—the youngest player in league history to surpass the fifteen-hundred-yard mark. In doing so he became the first Cowboy ever to lead the league, a feat that runners such as Tony Dorsett, Don Perkins, Calvin Hill, and Herschel Walker had failed to achieve.

Smith's playoff debut was also impressive. Playing the Chicago Bears, Emmitt raced for 105 yards in Dallas's 17-13 victory. In

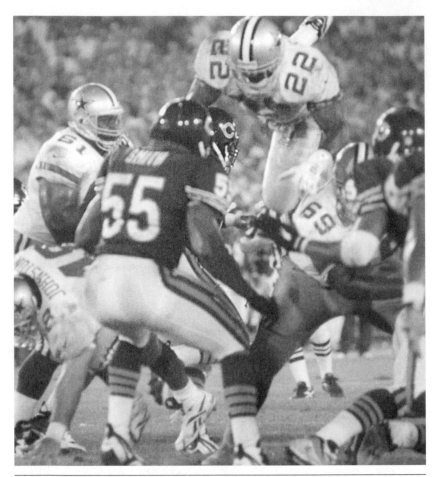

Smith (22) became the first player since 1932 to accumulate over 100 yards against the Chicago Bears in a playoff game.

twenty seven playoff games dating back to 1932, it was the first time the Bears had allowed a runner to break the hundred-yard barrier against them. Unfortunately, the Cowboys' hopes for a championship came crashing down the next week when they were "whupped" by the Detroit Lions, 38-6.

Super Bowl Success

The 1992 season was memorable for both the Cowboys and Smith. The team won its first divisional title since 1985, winning a franchise-record thirteen games against only three defeats. Smith shone from the running back position, winning another rushing title with 1,713 yards gained. This made him the first player to win back-to-back rushing crowns since Eric Dickerson of the Los Angeles Rams in 1984.

The Cowboys continued to win in the playoffs. They defeated the San Francisco 49ers in the NFC Championship game to advance to Super Bowl XXVII, where they met the AFC-champion Buffalo Bills. Buffalo proved to be no match for Dallas. The Cowboys forced nine Bills' turnovers and won by a score of 52-17. It was the Bills' third Super Bowl loss in as many years. Smith ran for 108 yards and scored a touchdown to earn his first championship ring. In the postgame locker room, he knew the feeling of accomplishment was something he would savor for a long time.

By the next spring, however, it appeared that team owner Jerry Jones had underestimated Smith's value to the team. Emmitt's original contract had been for three years and approximately $3 million. With two rushing titles and three Pro Bowl appearances in his first three seasons, Smith believed he should be paid more than any other running back in the league. Jones disagreed. "You're lucky to be a Dallas Cowboy," he told his star. "This is America's Team. Everyone wants that association. You should be proud to be part of America's Team."[104] Emmitt was proud, but he was also willing to stand up for what he believed in.

When Jones finally made an offer, it was far below Smith's expectations. The 1993 season began with Emmitt holding out. It took losses in the team's first two games before Jones began serious negotiations. Soon after, Smith signed a new four-year deal for $13.6 million. He joined the team in time for the third game of the season.

No team had ever lost its first two games and bounced back to win a Super Bowl, until the Cowboys did it in 1993. In the final game of the regular season they defeated the New York Giants 16-13 in overtime to win the division championship. Smith carried the ball thirty-two times for 168 yards and caught ten passes for another sixty-one yards. Incredibly, he played the second half with a separated shoulder. The *Dallas Morning News* called it "one of the best performances in Cowboys history,"[105] and no one disagreed.

In leading the Cowboys to another division title, Smith won his third rushing crown in a row, becoming just the fourth man in league history to perform the feat. Remarkably, he won the title despite missing the first two games of the season due to the contract dispute. A week after the Giants game Smith was rewarded for his efforts, becoming the first Dallas Cowboy to be named the NFL's Most Valuable Player.

The Cowboys defeated the San Francisco 49ers 38-21 to take the NFC championship, and moved on to Super Bowl XXVIII where their opponent once again was the Buffalo Bills. With the Cowboys losing 13-6 at halftime, Smith approached Norv Turner. "Norv," he said, "I need the ball in my hands more."[106] Turner agreed, and the second half saw Dallas dominate play. The Cowboys put twenty-four unanswered points on the board to walk away with a 30-13 win and a second consecutive Super Bowl championship. All Smith did was rush for 132 yards and score a pair of touchdowns. His most satisfying season ended with him being named the Most Valuable Player of the Super Bowl.

Continued Excellence

Following the Super Bowl victory, Dallas offensive coordinator Norv Turner left to take the head coaching position with the Washington Redskins. A clash of egos led to a parting of the ways between Cowboys coach Jimmy Johnson and owner Jerry Jones in late March. Barry Switzer was hired as the new head man, but the changing of the guard did not seem to affect Smith. After undergoing surgery in the off-season to repair his damaged shoulder, he bounced back to gain 1,484 yards on the ground. However, a series of nagging injuries continued to bother him throughout the year. He led the league with twenty-two touchdowns, and, incredibly, fumbled the ball just one time in 386 carries and fifty pass receptions. The Cowboys fell short in their bid for a third straight Super Bowl when the San Francisco 49ers defeated them in the NFC title game.

Everything came together for both the Cowboys and Smith in 1995. In the first game of the year against the New York Giants, Emmitt ran for a sixty-yard touchdown the first time he touched the ball. It was an omen of things to come. Smith cracked the hundred-yard mark eleven times while collecting a career-best

1,773 yards on the ground to win his fourth rushing title. He also set an NFL mark for touchdowns in a season with twenty-five. Emmitt led the league in scoring (150 points), total yards from scrimmage (2,148), and rushing attempts (377). His sixty-two pass receptions were another career best for him.

Smith continued his production in the playoffs. He rushed for 150 yards and scored three touchdowns in the NFC title game win over the Green Bay Packers. He ran for two more scores in Dallas's 27-17 victory over the Pittsburgh Steelers in Super Bowl XXX. It gave Emmitt his third championship ring in his sixth NFL season.

Smith was scheduled to become a free agent after the 1996 season. Cowboys owner Jerry Jones knew he could not afford to let Emmitt leave. In August he signed Smith to a new $42.5 million, eight-year contract, that included a $10.5 million signing bonus.

Smith (22) and Michael Irvin hoist the NFC title trophy, won after Smith rushed for 150 yards against the Green Bay Packers.

Since Emmitt signed his new deal, the Cowboys have not been able to make it back to the Super Bowl. The team has compiled two winning seasons (1996 and 1998), one .500 season (1999), and two losing seasons (1997 and 2000).

Despite being beset by several injuries, Smith has continued his assault on the league record book with his usual consistent play. As Nate Newton once said, "Emmitt Smith is like the mailman. Rain or shine, he always delivers." [107] Smith surpassed the thousand-yard mark in rushing every season, bringing his streak of consecutive years to ten to tie Barry Sanders' record. He is the third-ranked rusher on the all-time list, trailing only Walter Payton and Sanders, and has surpassed the hundred-yard mark in 71 of 172 career games. In 1998 he became the league's all-time leader in rushing touchdowns and stands second to Jerry Rice in total touchdowns.

Smith's value to the Cowboys can be summed up in one telling statistic: When he has carried the ball twenty or more times in a game, the Cowboys have won eighty-eight times and lost only nineteen (including playoffs). As coach Dave Campo said, "In the era of the '90s, the one single thing that made us successful probably more than any other was the selection of Emmitt Smith [in the 1990 draft]." [108]

The Future

Smith has proven to be the most durable of Dallas's famed "triplets" of the 1990s (as they were dubbed by Jerry Jones). Wide receiver Michael Irvin suffered a neck injury that forced him to retire following the 1999 season, while fear of the effect of repeated concussions caused the Cowboys to release quarterback Troy Aikman in early 2001.

Smith, however, continues to chase Walter Payton's all-time rushing mark of 16,726 yards. His skills have shown little sign of diminishing. If he continues at his current pace he will probably break the record sometime in 2002, which would be a testament to his reliability and durability. As Emmitt said following the 2000 season, "The only thing I can say about my consistency and my endurance is I've had my share of injuries just like any other player. . . . I think God has blessed me with some grace and some mercy to continue to play at a level that I've been able to play for eleven years now and hopefully many more years to come." [109]

Passing Tony Dorsett on the NFL all-time rushing list, Smith trails only Barry Sanders and Walter Payton.

Smith has always shown an appreciation for the gifts he has been given. He has tried to set a good example for youngsters, stressing the importance of getting an education. Although he left college early, he fulfilled a promise to his mother by returning to school to get his degree in public recreation from the College of Health and Human Performances at the University of Florida in May 1996. "It only takes a little time to make a significant difference in the lives of young people," said Emmitt. "I plan to help others with my degree. If we can reach just a few kids and let them know that education is a wonderful and necessary thing in today's workplace, then we will have been successful."[110]

Emmitt has earned the respect of others by giving back much to the community. In 1986 he represented the nation's prep football players at the White House as part of the "Just Say No" campaign to fight drugs. He founded Emmitt Smith Charities to help provide educational scholarships for underprivileged youngsters in his hometown of Pensacola. He also donates much of his time to a variety of causes such as the United Way, the Make A Wish Foundation, the Salvation Army, the American Lung Association, and the Battered and Abused Children's Foundation.

Smith's behavior on and off the field has made him a favorite of fans across the country and won him the respect of his peers. As Washington Redskins cornerback Darrell Green said when asked about Smith's assault on Payton's career rushing mark, "I think it would be great. All records will be broken in time, and I think Emmitt has been a class act for a long time. I would be the first guy to congratulate him." [111]

Emmitt believes he still has several years of productive play left to give to his team. "I'm moved by the opportunity to win," he said, "the opportunity to keep playing at the level I've established. I'm still chasing my place in history." [112] If he maintains reasonably good health, that place will be with the sport's other immortals in the Pro Football Hall of Fame in Canton, Ohio.

Notes

Chapter 1: America's Team

1. Quoted in Bill Campbell, "Underdog Image Helped Club Become 'America's Team,'" *Dallas Morning News*, September 9, 1999. www.dallasnews.com/sports_day/football/classic-cowboys/40americateam.htm.
2. Quoted in Campbell, "Underdog Image Helped Club Become 'America's Team.'"
3. Quoted in Campbell, "Underdog Image Helped Club Become 'America's Team.'"
4. Quoted in William Oscar Johnson, " 'A Chapter Closed,'" *Sports Illustrated*, March 6, 1989, p. 23.
5. Quoted in *The Sporting News*, "The 'Boys Are Back," January 31, 1993. www.sportingnews.com/archives/superbowl/27.html.
6. Quoted in Jean-Jacques Taylor, "Jones Says He's Spent Wisely," *Dallas Morning News*, January 11, 2001. www.dallasnews.com/sports_day/football/cowboys/cowboys/259051_cowlede_11spo..html.

Chapter 2: Tom Landry

7. Quoted in Cathy Harasta, "Opponents Remember," *Dallas Morning News*, March 12, 1989. www.dallasnews.com/specials/landryspecial/landryopp.htm.
8. Quoted in Tom Landry with Gregg Lewis, *Tom Landry: An Autobiography*. Grand Rapids, MI: Zondervan Publishing House, 1990, p. 50.
9. Quoted in Chip Brown, "Leading the Texas Troops," *Dallas Morning News*. www.dallasnews.com/specials/landryspecial/landryut.htm.
10. Quoted in Landry with Lewis, *Tom Landry*, p. 87.
11. Quoted in Mark Stein, "Giant Start," Dallas Morning News. www.dallasnews.com/specials/landryspecial/landrygiants.htm.

12. Quoted in Landry with Lewis, *Tom Landry*, p. 112.
13. Quoted in David Moore, "Building America's Team," *Dallas Morning News*. www.dallasnews.com/specials/landryspecial/landrybuild.htm.
14. Quoted in Paul Zimmerman, "Tom Landry: 1924-2000," *Sports Illustrated*, February 21, 2000, p. 76.
15. Quoted in Moore, "Building America's Team."
16. Quoted in Moore, "Building America's Team."
17. Quoted in Moore, "Building America's Team."
18. Quoted in Moore, "Building America's Team."
19. Quoted in Moore, "Building America's Team."
20. Quoted in Moore, "Building America's Team."
21. Quoted in Jean-Jacques Taylor, "Following the Leader," *Dallas Morning News*. www.dallasnews.com/specials/landryspecial/landryasststory.htm.
22. Quoted in *NFL.com*, "Tom Landry: The Present and Legacy." www.nfl.com/Cowboys/news/981015landry2.html.
23. Quoted in Harasta, "Opponents Remember."
24. Quoted in *CBS News*, "Legendary Coach Landry Dead." www.cbsnews.com/now/story/0,1597,146178-412,00.shtml.

Chapter 3: Bob Lilly

25. Quoted in Matt Moss, "Distant Replay: Bob Lilly," *NFL.com*. www.nfl.com/Cowboys/news/distantreplaylilly.html.
26. Quoted in Pete Golenbock, *Cowboys Have Always Been My Heroes*. New York: Warner Books, 1997, p. 140.
27. Quoted in Le Templar, "All-Pro Lilly Arrives in City," *Witchita Falls* (Texas) *Times Record News*, July 23, 1998. www.cowboyscamp.com/news/072398/lilly.html.
28. Quoted in Dave Anderson, *The Story of Football*. New York: Morrow, 1997, p. 133.
29. Quoted in Anderson, *The Story of Football*, 1997, p. 133.
30. Quoted in Golenbock, *Cowboys Have Always Been My Heroes*, p. 145.
31. Quoted in Ronald L. Mendell and Timothy B. Phares, *Who's Who in Football*. New Rochelle, NY: Arlington House, 1974, p. 199.
32. Quoted in Golenbock, *Cowboys Have Always Been My Heroes*, p. 236.
33. Quoted in Golenbock, *Cowboys Have Always Been My Heroes*, pp. 233–234.

34. Quoted in Golenbock, *Cowboys Have Always Been My Heroes*, p. 326.
35. Quoted in Golenbock, *Cowboys Have Always Been My Heroes*, p. 462.
36. Quoted in Nick Gholson, "Bob Lilly Finds Fulfillment Outside of Football," *Wichita Falls* (Texas) *Times Record News*, December 22, 1998. www.poncacitynews.com/NewsArchives/1298folder/lo122298.html.
37. Quoted in Le Templar, "All-Pro Lilly Arrives in City."
38. Quoted in Golenbock, *Cowboys Have Always Been My Heroes*, p. 576.
39. Quoted in Peter King, *Football: A History of the Professional Game*. New York: Time, 1996, p. 122.
40. Quoted in Gholson, "Bob Lilly Finds Fulfillment Outside of Football."
41. Quoted in Gholson, "Bob Lilly Finds Fulfillment Outside of Football."
42. Quoted in Gholson, "Bob Lilly Finds Fulfillment Outside of Football."
43. Quoted in Scott Pitoniak, "Lilly Says Cowboys Would Make Mistake in Taking Moss," *Rochester Democrat and Chronicle*. detnews.com/1998/sports/9804/17/04170065.htm.

Chapter 4: Bob Hayes

44. Quoted in Joey Johnston, "Yesterday's Heroes," *Football Digest*, May/June 1987, p. 86.
45. Quoted in Gene Frenette, "Number One with a 'Bullet,'" *Florida Times-Union*. www.jacksonville.com/special/athletes_of_century/stories/hayes.shtml.
46. Quoted in Charles Moritz, ed., *Current Biography Yearbook: 1966*. New York: The H. W. Wilson Co., 1966, p. 163.
47. Quoted in Bob Hayes with Robert Pack, *Run, Bullet, Run*. New York: Harper & Row, Publishers, 1990, p. 104.
48. Hayes with Pack, *Run, Bullet, Run*. New York: Harper & Row, 1990, p. 106.
49. Quoted in Hayes with Pack, *Run, Bullet, Run*, p. 106.
50. Quoted in Hayes with Pack, *Run, Bullet, Run*, p. 159.
51. Quoted in Randy Galloway, "Hall of Fame Plaque Now Lawrence Taylor–Made for Bob Hayes," *Fort Worth Star-Telegram*.www.texnews.com/1998/1999/cowboys/randy0301.html.

52. Quoted in Johnston, "Yesterday's Heroes," p. 84.

53. Quoted in Johnston, "Yesterday's Heroes," p. 88.

54. Quoted in Ernest Hooper, "Dallas Honor Reconsidered," *St. Petersburg Times*, August 27, 2000. web2.sptimes.com/News/082700/Sports/Dallas_honor_reconsid.shtml.

55. Quoted in *Sportsline*, "Hayes in Fair Condition after Prostate Surgery," March 6, 2001. web1.sportsline.com/u/ce/multi/0,1329,3612137_59,00.html.

Chapter 5: Roger Staubach

56. Quoted in Gene Wojciechowski, "Roger Staubach is Inducted into the Pro Football Hall of Fame," *Dallas Morning News*, August 4, 1985. www.dallasnews.com/sports_day/football/classic cowboys/1029classic.htm.

57. Quoted in Charles Moritz, ed., *Current Biography Yearbook: 1972*. New York: The H. W. Wilson Co., 1972, p. 410.

58. Quoted in *CNN/Sports Illustrated*, "Roger Staubach (1963): Heisman Heroes." 207.25.71.142/football/college/heisman/0903/.

59. Quoted in Golenbock, *Cowboys Have Always Been My Heroes*, p. 463.

60. Quoted in Golenbock, *Cowboys Have Always Been My Heroes*, p. 491.

61. Quoted in Golenbock, *Cowboys Have Always Been My Heroes*, p. 492.

62. Quoted in Golenbock, *Cowboys Have Always Been My Heroes*, p. 498.

63. Quoted in Golenbock, *Cowboys Have Always Been My Heroes*, p. 551.

64. Quoted in Golenbock, *Cowboys Have Always Been My Heroes*, p. 595.

65. Quoted in Bob St. John, "Can You Believe Those Cowboys?" *Dallas Morning News*, December 29, 1975. www.dallasnews.com/sports_day/football/classiccowboys/hailmary/1228stjohn.htm.

66. Quoted in St. John, "Can You Believe Those Cowboys?"

67. Quoted in *The American Enterprise* " 'Live' with TAE: Roger Staubach," www.theamericanenterprise.org/taeon00b.htm.

68. Quoted in Carlton Stowers, "Roger Hangs 'Em Up," *Dallas Morning News*, April 1, 1980. www.dallasnews.com/sports_day/football/classiccowboys/0328roger1.htm.

69. Quoted in Hayes with Pack, *Run, Bullet, Run*, p. 288.
70. Quoted in *Famous Texans*, "Football Star Turned Business Titan." www.famoustexans.com/rogerstaubach.htm.
71. Quoted in Sam Blair, "Landry's QB Succession Left Indelible Impression," *Dallas Morning News*, August 1, 1990. www.dallas news.com/sports_day/football/classiccowboys/1202landryq bs.htm.
72. Quoted in Hayes with Pack, *Run, Bullet, Run*, pp. 288–89.

Chapter 6: Tony Dorsett

73. Quoted in Tony Dorsett and Harvey Frommer, *Running Tough*. New York: Doubleday, 1989, p. 6.
74. Quoted in Dorsett and Frommer, *Running Tough*, p. 7.
75. Quoted in Dorsett and Frommer, *Running Tough*, p. 13.
76. Quoted in Dorsett and Frommer, *Running Tough*, p. 22.
77. Quoted in Golenbock, *Cowboys Have Always Been My Heroes*, p. 617.
78. Quoted in Dorsett and Frommer, *Running Tough*, pp. 25–26.
79. Quoted in Golenbock, *Cowboys Have Always Been My Heroes*, p. 617.
80. Quoted in Dorsett and Frommer, *Running Tough*, p. 52.
81. Quoted in Golenbock, *Cowboys Have Always Been My Heroes*, p. 622.
82. Quoted in Dorsett and Frommer, *Running Tough*, p. 119.
83. Quoted in Paul Zimmerman, "Goodbye Big D, Hello Denver," *Sports Illustrated*, August 1, 1988, p. 38.
84. Quoted in *National Football League*, "An Intense Competitor." www.nfl.com/news/greatest/dorsett.html.
85. Quoted in Clarence E. Hill Jr., "His Records Will Fall, but Tony D. Got His Groove Back," *Fort Worth Star-Telegram*, November 22, 1998. www.reporternews.com/texsports/td1122.html.
86. Quoted in Hill, "His Records Will Fall, but Tony D. Got His Groove Back."

Chapter 7: Troy Aikman

87. Quoted in Jill Lieber, "Most Visible Player," *Sports Illustrated*, February 15, 1993, p. 29.
88. Quoted in The Staff of Beckett Publications, *Beckett Great Sports Heroes: Troy Aikman*. New York: House of Collectibles, 1996, p. 68.

89. Quoted in Beckett Publications, *Troy Aikman*, p. 74.
90. Quoted in Lieber, "Most Visible Player," p. 29.
91. Quoted in Beckett Publications, *Troy Aikman*, p. 44.
92. Quoted in Beckett Publications, *Troy Aikman*, p. 19.
93. Quoted in Beckett Publications, *Troy Aikman*, p. 23.
94. Quoted in Beckett Publications, *Troy Aikman*, p.127.
95. Quoted in Jim Reeves, "Aikman Passed Tough Decision to Jones," *Fort Worth Star-Telegram*, March 8, 2001. www.reporter news.com/2001/cowboys/tough0308.html.
96. Quoted in Jaime Aron, "Big Bonus Forces Cowboys to Waive Aikman," *Abilene Reporter-News*, March 8, 2001. www.reporter news.com/2001/cowboys/gib0308.html.
97. Quoted in Aron, "Big Bonus Forces Cowboys to Waive Aikman."

Chapter 8: Emmitt Smith

98. Emmitt Smith with Steve Delsohn, *The Emmitt Zone*. Dallas: Taylor Publishing Co., 1995, p. 29.
99. Smith with Delsohn, *The Emmitt Zone*, p. 27.
100. Quoted in Austin Murphy, *The Super Bowl: Sports' Greatest Championship*. New York: Time, 1998, p. 129.
101. Quoted in Smith with Delsohn, *The Emmitt Zone*, p. 69.
102. Quoted in Smith with Delsohn, *The Emmitt Zone*, p. 106.
103. Quoted in Smith with Delsohn, *The Emmitt Zone*, p. 106.
104. Quoted in Smith with Delsohn, *The Emmitt Zone*, p. 209.
105. Quoted in Smith with Delsohn, *The Emmitt Zone*, p. 243.
106. Quoted in Smith with Delsohn, *The Emmitt Zone*, p. 256.
107. Quoted in Golenbock, *Cowboys Have Always Been My Heroes*, p. 780.
108. Quoted in Charean Williams, "Last Man Standing," *Football Digest*, March 2001.
109. Quoted in Williams, "Last Man Standing."
110. Quoted in *Associated Press*, "Emmitt Smith to Graduate from Florida Saturday," April 30, 1996. www.texnews.com/cowboys/emmitt043096.html.
111. Quoted in Williams, "Last Man Standing."
112. Quoted in Jean-Jacques Taylor, "Ageless Wonder Emmitt Smith, 31, Still Chasing Place in History," *Abilene Reporter-News*, August 24, 2000. www.reporternews.com/2000/cowboys/emm0824.html.

For Further Reading

Gene Brown, ed., *The New York Times Encyclopedia of Sports: Football.* New York: Arno Press, 1979. A collection of articles from the *New York Times* tracing the history of football from 1905 to 1979.

Bob Carroll, *100 Greatest Running Backs.* New York: Crescent Books, 1989. Looks at the workhorses who grind out the yards and put points on the board.

Bob Carroll et al., eds., *Total Football.* New York: HarperCollins, 1997. Comprehensive football reference containing statistics and historical essays.

John Eisenberg, *Cotton Bowl Days: Growing Up with Dallas and the Cowboys in the 1960s.* New York: Contemporary Books, 2000. A look at the city of Dallas in the 1960s through the eyes of a life-long Cowboys fan.

Hank Hersch, *Greatest Football Games of All Time.* New York: Time, 1997. *Sports Illustrated* series volume that examines pro football's all-time classic games.

Howie Long, *Football for Dummies.* New York: Hungry Minds, 1998. This volume in the *for Dummies* series examines every aspect of football, including plays, positions, and strategy.

David S. Neft and Richard Cohen, *The Sports Encyclopedia: Pro Football.* New York: St. Martin's Press, 1987. Definitive statistical history of professional football in the modern era, from 1960 to 1986.

Richard Whittingham, *The Fireside Book of Pro Football.* New York: Simon & Schuster, 1989. Collection of writings on professional football.

Works Consulted

Books

Dave Anderson, *The Story of Football*. New York: Morrow, 1997. Pulitzer Prize–winning sportswriter updates his 1985 version of the history of the game.

Tony Dorsett and Harvey Frommer, *Running Tough*. New York: Doubleday, 1989. Autobiography of the 1976 Heisman Trophy winner and one of the NFL's all-time rushing greats.

Pete Golenbock, *Cowboys Have Always Been My Heroes*. New York: Warner Books, 1997. This eight-hundred-page volume is the definitive oral history of the Dallas Cowboys.

Bob Hayes with Robert Pack, *Run, Bullet, Run*. New York: Harper & Row, 1990. The candid autobiography of Bob Hayes, the world's fastest man.

Peter King, *Football: A History of the Professional Game*. New York: Time, 1996. *Sports Illustrated* series volume that is an authoritative tribute to America's most popular sport.

Tom Landry with Gregg Lewis, *Tom Landry: An Autobiography*. Grand Rapids, MI: Zondervan Publishing House, 1990. The autobiography of Tom Landry, the man who was the Dallas Cowboys.

Ronald L. Mendell and Timothy B. Phares, *Who's Who in Football*. New Rochelle, NY: Arlington House, 1974. This book contains over fourteen hundred biographical sketches of football players, coaches, officials, and administrators.

Charles Moritz, ed., *Current Biography Yearbook: 1966*. New York: The H. W. Wilson Co., 1966. Library volume that contains all of the biographies published in the *Current Biography* magazine in 1966.

Charles Moritz, ed., *Current Biography Yearbook: 1972*. New York: The H. W. Wilson Co., 1972. Library volume that contains all of the biographies published in the *Current Biography* magazine in 1972.

Austin Murphy, *The Super Bowl: Sports' Greatest Championship.* New York: Time, 1998. This volume in the lavishly illustrated series of *Sports Illustrated* books chronicles the history of the Super Bowl along with the stars of the games.

Emmitt Smith with Steve Delsohn, *The Emmitt Zone.* Dallas: Taylor Publishing Co., 1995. The autobiography of Emmitt Smith, the Cowboys star running back of the 1990s.

The Staff of Beckett Publications, *Beckett Great Sports Heroes: Troy Aikman.* New York: House of Collectibles, 1996. This biography of Cowboys quarterback Tony Aikman includes many full-color photographs.

Periodicals

William Oscar Johnson, "'A Chapter Closed,'" *Sports Illustrated,* March 6, 1989.

Joey Johnston, "Yesterday's Heroes," *Football Digest,* May/June 1987.

Jill Lieber, "Most Visible Player," *Sports Illustrated,* February 15, 1993.

Charean Williams, "Last Man Standing," *Football Digest,* March 2001.

Paul Zimmerman, "Goodbye Big D, Hello Denver," *Sports Illustrated,* August 1, 1988.

Paul Zimmerman, "Tom Landry: 1924–2000," *Sports Illustrated,* February 21, 2000.

Internet Sources

The American Enterprise, "'Live' with TAE: Roger Staubach." www.theamericanenterprise.org/taeon00b.htm.

Jaime Aron, "Big Bonus Forces Cowboys to Waive Aikman," *Abilene Reporter-News,* March 8, 2001. www.reporternews.com/2001/cowboys/gib0308.html.

Quoted in *Associated Press,* "Emmitt Smith to Graduate from Florida Saturday," April 30, 1996. www.texnews.com/cowboys/emmitt043096html.

Sam Blair, "Landry's QB Succession Left Indelible Impression," *Dallas Morning News,* August 1, 1990. www.dallasnews.com/sports_day/football/classiccowboys/1202landryqbs.htm.

Chip Brown, "Leading the Texas Troops," *Dallas Morning News.* www.dallasnews.com/specials/landryspecial/landryut.htm.

Bill Campbell, "Underdog Image Helped Club Become 'America's Team,'" *Dallas Morning News.* www.dallasnews.com/sports_day/football/classiccowboys/40americateam.htm.

CBS News, "Legendary Coach Landry Dead." www.cbsnews.com/now/story/0,1597,146178-412,000.stml.

CNN/*Sports Illustrated,* "Roger Staubach (1963): Heisman Heroes." www.reporternews.com/2001/cowboys/tough0308.html.

Famous Texans, "Football Star Turned Business Titan." www.famoustexans.com/rogerstaubach.htm.

Gene Frenette, "Number One with a 'Bullet,'" *Florida Times-Union.* www.jacksonville.com/special/athletes_of_century/stories/hayes.shtml.

Randy Galloway, "Hall of Fame Plaque Now Lawrence Taylor–Made for Bob Hayes," *Fort Worth Star-Telegram.* www.texnews.com/1998/1999/cowboys/randy0301.html.

Nick Gholson, "Bob Lilly Finds Fulfillment Outside of Football," *Wichita Falls* (Texas) *Times Record News,* December 22, 1998. www.poncacitynews.com/NewsArchives/1298folder/lo122298.html.

Cathy Harasta, "Opponents Remember." *Dallas Morning News.* www.dallasnews.com/specials/landryspecial/landryopp.htm.

Clarence E. Hill Jr., "His Records Will Fall, but Tony D. Got His Groove Back," *Fort Worth Star-Telegram,* November 22, 1998. www.reporternews.com/texsports/td1122.html.

Ernest Hooper, "Dallas Honor Reconsidered," *St. Petersburg Times,* August 27, 2000. web2.sptimes.com/News/082700/Sports/Dallas_honor_reconsid.shtml.

David Moore, "Building America's Team," *Dallas Morning News.* www.dallasnews.com/specials/landryspecial/landrybuild.htm.

Matt Moss, "Distant Replay: Bob Lilly," NFL.com. www.nfl.com/Cowboys/news/distantreplaylilly.html.

National Football League, "An Intense Competitor." www.nfl.com/news/greatest/dorsett.html.

NFL.com, "Tom Landry: The Present and Legacy." www.nfl.com/Cowboys/news/981015landry2.html.

Scott Pitoniak, "Lilly Says Cowboys Would Make Mistake in Taking Moss," *Rochester Democrat and Chronicle.* detnews.com/1998/sports/9804/17/04170065.htm.

Jim Reeves, "Aikman Passed Tough Decision to Jones," *Fort Worth Star-Telegram,* March 8, 2001. www.reporternews.com/2001/cowboys/tough0308.html.

The Sporting News, "The 'Boys Are Back." www.sportingnews.com/archives/superbowl/27.html.

Sportsline, "Hayes in Fair Condition after Prostate Surgery," March 6, 2001. web1.sportsline.com/u/ce/multi/0,1329,3612137_59,00.html.

Bob St. John, "Can You Believe Those Cowboys?" *Dallas Morning News,* December 29, 1975. www.dallasnews.com/sports_day/football/classiccowboys/hailmary/1228stjohn.htm.

Mark Stein, "Giant Start," *Dallas Morning News.* www.dallasnews.com/specials/landryspecial/landrygiants.htm.

Carlton Stowers, "Roger Hangs 'Em Up," *Dallas Morning News,* April 1, 1980. www.dallasnews.com/sports_day/football/classiccowboys/0328roger1.htm.

Jean-Jacques Taylor, "Ageless Wonder Emmitt Smith, 31, Still Chasing Place in History," *Abilene Reporter-News,* August 24, 2000. www.reporternews.com/2000/cowboys/emm0824.html.

Jean-Jacques Taylor, "Following the Leader," *Dallas Morning News.* www.dallasnews.com/specials/landryspecial/landryasststory.htm.

Jean-Jacques Taylor, "Jones Says He's Spent Wisely," *Dallas Morning News,* January 11, 2001. www.dallasnews.com/sports_day/football/cowboys/cowboys/259051_cowlede_11spo..html.

Le Templar, "All-Pro Lilly Arrives in City," *Wichita Falls* (Texas) *Times Record News,* July 23, 1998. www.cowboyscamp.com/news/072398/lilly.html.

Gene Wojciechowski, "Roger Staubach Is Inducted into the Pro Football Hall of Fame," *Dallas Morning News,* August 4, 1985. www.dallasnews.com/sports_day/football/classiccowboys/1029classic.htm.

Web Sites

The Dallas Morning News–(www.dallasnews.com) Website of the
Dallas newspaper.

The National Football League–(www.nfl.com) Website of the
National Football League.

Texnews–(www.texnews.com) Website of the *Abilene Reporter-News*/Texnews Network.

Index

Picture Credits

About the Author

John F. Grabowski is a native of Brooklyn, New York. He holds a bachelor's degree in psychology from City College of New York and a master's degree in educational psychology from Teacher's College, Columbia University. He has been a teacher for thirty-one years as well as a freelance writer, specializing in the fields of sports, education, and comedy. His body of published work includes thirty books; a nationally syndicated sports column; consultation on several math textbooks; articles for newspapers, magazines, and the programs of professional sports teams; and comedy material sold to Jay Leno, Joan Rivers, Yakov Smirnoff, and numerous other comics. He and his wife Patricia live in Staten Island with their daughter Elizabeth.

This book belongs to...

_____